Olympic Weightlifting Strength Manual

Picture, Thomas Barry

Olympic Weightlifting Strength Manual
by Louie Simmons
Writer: Louie Simmons
Editor: Doris Simmons and Martha C. Johnson
Photography editor: Thomas Barry
Publisher: Westside Barbell
Covers and layout: Scott D Web Graphics®
Printer: Action Printing, Inc. Wisconsin
Copyright © Westside Barbell, Louie Simmons 2016
No part of this book may be reproduced in any form or by any means without the
prior written consent of the publisher. Except of the brief quotes used in reviews.
Disclaimer: The author and publisher of this material are not responsible in any manner whatsoever
for any injury that may occur through following the instructions contained in this material.
The activities may be too strenuous or dangerous for some people. The readers should
always consult a physician before engaging in them.

Foreword

My knowledge of special strength training came from many Soviet scientists and coaches whom I commend for their tireless efforts to find the real truth about training for all sports. I was greatly influenced by V.M. Zatsiorsky, Y.V. Verkhoshansky, A.S. Medvedyev, R.A. Roman, N.P. Laputin, V.G. Oleshko, and L.S. Dvorkin for their insights on all special methods of training, especially the conjugate system that connects all methods.

For loading, three special men A.D. Ermakov, N.S. Atanasov, and A.S. Prilepin were critical to my success. For calculating periodization, Arosiev-Vorobev and Ermakov provided complete understanding on the division between maximal effort, explosive and speed training. Also, a special thanks goes to Dr. Mel Siff for spending so much time at Westside Barbell discussing training philosophies.

It is easy to see the light when standing on the shoulders of giants.

Louie Simmons

TABLE OF CONTENTS

Foreword		iii
Table of Contents		v
Dedication		xvii
Introduction		1
Chapter 1:	**Fixing Today's Lifting Programs**	3
	Recruiting Young People	3
	Accommodation	6
	Western Periodization	7
	Coaching	7
	Training Methods	7
	Technique Errors	8
	A Different Future	9
Chapter 2:	**Special Squats**	15
	Let's Look At A Different Method	15
	First—Box Squats	15
	Belt Squats	16
	Power Rack Squats—Shock Methods	16
	Note: Strength Potential	16
	Why!	17
	Special Exercises	17
	Small Special Exercises	17
	Large Special Exercises	17
	The Key	18
	Small Special Exercise Examples	18
Chapter 3:	**Speed Strength Training**	23
	Power Snatch from the Floor	23
	Power Snatch from Below the Knee	23
	Snatch with Bar Below the Knee (Squat Style)	23
	Snatch with Bar Above the Knee (Squat Style)	23
Chapter 4:	**Methods**	27
	Maximal Effort Method	28
	Dynamic Effort Method	29
	Submaximal and Repeated Effort Method	30
Chapter 5:	**Increasing Explosive Strength through Plyometrics**	35
	Are Depth Jumps and Bounding Safe?	35
	The Dynamic Method	36
	Maximal Effort Method	36
	The Repetition Method	36
	Basic Jump Program	36

TABLE OF CONTENTS

	Explosive Weight Jumps	37
	Depth Jumps	37
	Depth Drops vs. Depth Jumps	37
	Dr. Verkhoshansky's Depth Jump Method	37
	How to Land	37
	The Takeoff Phase	38
	Westside Use of Depth Jumps	38
	Recommended Reading	38
Chapter 6:	**Periodization Division Into Training Periods**	43
	Three-Week Speed Strength Wave	43
	Volume and Intensity Zones	43
	Four Direct Periods of Periodization	46
	The Importance of Observation	46
	Eliminating Accommodation	46
	Nine-Week Training Cycle	47
	More Wave Cycle Discussion	51
	Monitoring Progress with the Westside System	52
	The Plan: From a 400- to a 1,000-Pound Squat	52
	Changing Volume While Maintaining Bar Speed	55
	Band Jerk and Press Workout for Speed Strength	56
	Periodization by Percentages	56
	Four Examples of a Three-Week Wave	59
	Speed Pulls	60
	Speed Pulls on Floor with Bands	60
	Ultra-wide Sumo Deadlifts with Bar Weight	61
	Box Deadlifts	61
	How to Change Volume at the Same Intensity Zone	65
	Circa Max	67
	Delayed Transformation Connecting Circa-Max Phase	67
	Workouts	68
	Special Notes	69
	Progress Is Based On Periodization	69
	Special Exercises	70
Chapter 7:	**Speed Strength and Max Effort Workouts**	75
	Speed Workouts	75
	Forty Three-Week Wave Examples	75
Chapter 8	**Special Notes**	97
	Periodization	97
	Avoiding Accommodation	98
	Final Instructions	98
	Programming	98
	Delayed Transformation	98
	Delayed Transmutation	98
	Training Session	99
	Squats	99

TABLE OF CONTENTS

Box Squatting	100
Equipment	101
Weightlifting Method of Those Strongest	102
The Chinese Method	102
Other Notes on Technique	104
The Soviet Method	104
The Bulgarian Method	105
The Westside System	106
Recruiting	108

Chapter 9: Special Exercises for Strength Development ... 113

Why Box Squats?	113
What is Correct Box Squatting?	113
Accommodating Resistance	113
Combining Resistance Methods	114
Bands	114
Misguiding the Barbell Trajectory	114
Leg Strength	114
Speed Strength Squat Workout	114
Examples, Exercise Illustrations	115
Large Exercises	117
Bent Over Row	118
Bow Bar Squat	120
Cambered Bar Squat	121
Clean Pull Standing on Mat	122
Clean ...;	124
Clean and Split Jerk	126
Snatch	130
Muscle Snatch	134
Cleans & Press Against Mini Bands (Single Strand)	136
Good Mornings with Safety Bar	142
Good Mornings with Safety Bar & Bands	144
Back Squats	146
Over Head Squats	148
Low Box Squat with Safety Squat Bar	152
Manta Ray	154
Clean From a 4-inch Box	156
Snatch From a 4-inch Box	158
Close Grip Snatch From a 4-inch Box	162
Concentric Squat	166
High Box Squat Into Overhead Press From Rack	170
Split Jerk From Pins	176
Russian Twists	180
High Pulls Narrow Grip	186
High Pulls Wide Grip	188
Power Snatch With Over Head Squat	190

TABLE OF CONTENTS

  Safety Bar Squat 192
  Shrugs Regular Grip 194
  Shrugs Wide Grip 196
  Single Hand Deadlift 198
  Single Handed Snatch 200
  Snatch From Box with Overhead Squat 204
  Push Press Plus Jerk from a Box 206
  Snatch From the Hang Position 208
  Static Squat 212
  Static Lunge Performed on the Westside Barbell Static/Dynamic Mach 214
  Static Squat Performed on the Westside Barbell Static/Dynamic Mach 215
  Static Front Squat Performed on the Westside B. Static/Dynamic Mach 215
  Straight Leg Deadlift 216
  Upright Row 219
  Zercher Squat 222
General Physical Preparedness (GPP) 229
  Sled 230
  Walking with a Safety Squat Bar 232
  Walking With Weight Vest 234
  Wheel Barrow 236
  Yolk Walk 238
Smaller Exercises 241
  Banded Hamstring Curls 242
  Barbell Twists 246
  Belt Squat Exercises 250
  Decline Bench Sit Ups 252
  Depth Jump 254
  Seated Box Jump 258
  Standing Box Jump 262
  Dips 266
  Glute Ham Back Extension With Sandbag 270
  Inverse Curl 274
  Belt Squat 280
  Belt Squat Cleans With Kettlebells 284
  Belt Squat Over Head Squat With Kettlebells 288
  Belt Squat Pull Throws (Variations 1 & 2) 292
  Plyo Swings 298
  Plyo Swings Leg Press with (Added Band) 304
  45 Degree Hyper 310
  Back Attack 316
  Hip - Ab Developer 323
  Lunge 324
  Lying Hamstring Curls 326
  Lying Leg Raise 328
  Pull Ups 330

TABLE OF CONTENTS

    Reverse Hyper 332
    Side Bends 334
    Single Leg Squat 336
    Standing Leg Curls 338
    Triceps Extensions 340
        Williams Press 346
Selected Bibliography & References 351

Dedication

This book is dedicated to all of my American weightlifting friends who represent the USA in the beautiful sport year in, year out. Westside has done extensive work in combining the Chinese, the former Soviet Union and the Westside system into a practical program to excel at the ultimate test of technique and strength. It will lead one from being a competent weightlifter to mastering weightlifting.

Louie Simmons

INTRODUCTION

WESTSIDE BARBELL

INTRODUCTION

I am writing this book on the development of special strengths to help raise individual lifts, specifically the snatch and the clean and jerk. The value of the top strength has been forgotten. If strength did not matter, then there would be no need for weight classes. But, indeed, there are weight classes and the weights are always larger in the next higher weight class.

Every discussion turns to technique in the classical lifts and special pulls. Great emphasis must be paid to technique in the early phases of training, hopefully, starting at age nine and up until 13-years-old. Basic specialization should occur at ages 14 to 15, specialization at ages 16 to 18, the phase of specialization at 19 to 20, and finally, the high performance stage, beginning at 21-years-old.

Whatever age, technique must be taught in the beginning. A basic long-range plan for weight lifting was used by many East Bloc countries like the German Democratic Republic (GDR), Poland, and Bulgaria, whose training was greatly influenced by the Russians. This is the technique I have followed with several young powerlifters. Kenny Patterson started at age 14 and was an open world record holder at 20-years-old. Joe McCoy started at 14 as well and was an open world champion at 19-years-old. David Hoff started at age 15 and has the all-time greatest powerlifting coefficient at 24-years-old.

The Westside system is basically from the former Soviet Union along with our own special exercises for powerlifting. Ninety-nine percent of the training advice comes from the translations of Andrew Charniga Jr. and his collection of weightlifting yearbooks plus many others. I paid great attention to the training of the strongest lifters from the Dynamo club. In an article by I.N Abramovsky in the 1985 yearbook entitled Dynamics of a Weightlifter, he states the most important quality of a weightlifter is strength. While the article is about moving up in a weight class to achieve new records, our top all-time female lifter has broken more than 30 all-time records in the same weight class. This shows that you don't have to gain weight to become stronger if your body structure is correct for your class.

An article by P.A Poleayev and V.S. Kopysov states that it is known that weightlifting achievements depend on the sportsman's strength potential, which is closely related to his bodyweight. They were not against gaining hypertrophy in the precise muscle groups. Yet again, it is strength potential which is closely related to the lifter's bodyweight. They were not against gaining hypertrophy in the precise muscle groups. Yet again, it is strength that limits a weightlifter's progress. As he grows into a higher weight class the strength increases, not just the technique, as it was developed in the early in his career.

I believe the constant discussion of technique is to camouflage the fact that they don't know how to make a person super strong.

The former Soviet Union had special exercises and special devices to increase strength. The Westside system also has special devices such as belt squat machines, inverse hamstring devices, Reverse Hypers™, plyo swings, and a static dynamic developer. Plus, Westside has numerous special exercises and bars to improve the strongest men and women's strength.

I hope you like this book and I hope you take the word "**Can't**" out of your vocabulary. You will find you indeed can raise the American flag on the Olympic stage once again. Sometimes to win, you must do the impossible, therefore, nothing is impossible.

Louie Simmons

Chapter 1: Fixing Today's Lifting Programs

Chapter 1: Fixing Today's Lifting Programs

There is a great interest in Olympic weightlifting in America, but since the press was abolished in 1972 we have unfortunately slipped far behind internationally. But this does not stop a small group of die-hards from continuing their best to compete at the international level with a dream of stepping on an international platform one day. I am afraid this will never happen due to the present coaching we have.

The talk is always about lifting technique or technique that is close to (if not equal to) our European brothers. Why then do we fail to make a high qualifying total that to them seems easy? It is due to their focus on absolute strength development in both classical lifts, but also including special exercises (not Olympic style lifts) for the back, large and small, as well as the leg squat, and special small exercises for the legs and torso. It is also due to their focused training programs. Before we get into the special strength training segment, a series of problems must be addressed and we must look at what it requires to make a strong national team.

Recruiting Young People

To create a strong national team the US needs to have a strong base of athletes from which to choose. We must follow the methods of the greatest teams in history. If we look at the former Soviet Union, they had five phases of training—Phase One can start at nine or 10 up to 13-years-old. This initial phase includes the rule of three where many sport activities are introduced into the child's program. For instance, among other Olympic style weightlifting, do they have the motor skills to learn the basic form such as overhead squat, full snatch, or front squat? They also must show interest in the sport of weightlifting, and the weightlifting community must recruit at this age. After all, other sports played with balls are popular; even boxing and wrestling have lots of young athletes to choose from. Why is that? These sports make the games enjoyable, with interaction while training or competing, music of their choosing, and a general fun atmosphere. After watching a documentary on American weightlifting, it seems the state of weightlifting in America is depressing at best. Being a powerlifter, I know that we listen to loud music and have lots of encouragement from training mates as well as involved spectators at contests. None of this happened in the documentary. THE IDEA THAT WEIGHTLIFING IS BORING MUST CHANGE NOW!

We must take the young boys and girls who don't like a team sport and entice them into a sport where you do the work and you get the full credit. The more the better as we know; the more engaged in a sport the better the odds some one great will emerge and shock the world. This is where technique is introduced. Here is where we first begin to master SWP (Special Weightlifting Preparation) and it is given top priority over GWP (General Weightlifting Preparation). If great attention is given to the 11- to 13-year-olds, the major motor systems of coordination are at a place where the ability to learn the basic skills are easiest. It is almost impossible to learn perfect technique after 13 because the ability to learn begins to decrease even at this early age. All of this is discussed in the book by Rick Brunner and Ben Tabachnik, PhD.

After the first phase and stage 2, the other four Soviet phases were:
- Basic specialization at ages 14 and 15
- Specialization at ages 16 and 18
- Phase of perfection at ages 19 and 20
- High performance phase at ages 21+

Many times our lifters have foreign foes, then the wide difference in totals show up. Why? It is lack of absolute strength. Back to recruiting, junior high teams across America must be formed, then high school teams and then college teams with money and tuition grants to entice more lifters not to go into other sports.

This is a new generation of people who need new stimulation. Don't be so sterile! We must use the current music to motivate the younger generation even at meets. Power meets use whatever music the lifter wants to hear on stage while they lift. Why can't the Olympic lifters do the same?

What other methods of training can make the hours of grueling work more fun? A wide variety of special equipment and bars is part of the answer.

Accommodation

When I watch Olympic lifting in its current state, I can only think of one thing: Accommodation. When doing the same training—using the same exercises over and over with the same volume or intensity—a lifter's performance will slow or even go backwards. It is common for US Olympic lifters to do only six exercises: power clean and snatch, the two classical lifts, and front and back squats. To use such pure exercises and succeed, the athlete must be very pure as well, meaning totally built for the two events. In the US, the expectation is that the result of exercise is always an increase in performance, but if nothing in the program is changed, the athlete experiences the principle of diminishing returns. This is a general law of biology and simply means if one does a constant stimulus, that stimulus will decrease over time. And that describes weightlifting today in a nutshell. Nothing changes, and of course, that includes your total. Remember in the beginning, young lifters will make progress with small training loads. One must increase the training loads as the lifts increase, so at some point in training progress will stop if new training stimulations are not introduced.

What other means and methods can be introduced to avoid accommodation? One is a large assortment of special bars and squats.

- Safety squat bar
- 14" cambered bar
- Bow bar
- Zercher squat
- Belt squat
- Box squat

Now the lifter has many bars to use and break records, which adds excitement as well. The belt squat can be a most valuable tool for an Olympic lifter, including holding a heavy medicine ball or doing power cleans while in the belt squat machine.

Speaking of machines, if you are making a goal of the world championships or the Olympics, not the county fair, you must have a:

- Calf/Glute ham
- Static Dynamic
- Reverse HyperTM
- 45-degree hyperextension
- Inverse curl bench
- Plyo swing
- Goodmorning machine

The above mentioned bars and training devices will be explained in the training routines later on. The Soviet Team, by the way, would use 100 special exercises for weightlifting.

Western Periodization

This style of cycling for a meet is the most outdated method, yet because no one seems to read about the subject, it continues. Westside uses a three-week pendulum wave. Using the old way, the author found that after three weeks he became no stronger or faster. Ironically Dr. Mel Siff said to the author that V. Alexeyev used the same three-week wave for the very same reasons.

The Westside system has a Max Effort (ME) day, a Dynamic Effort (DE) day for explosive or speed strength, plus a ratio of 80 percent special exercises to 20 percent classical exercises for hypertrophy in a weekly plan, which is constantly rotated throughout a weekly, monthly, and year-long plan leading to a multi-year plan. The Olympic lifter must adapt the system to make continuous progress year after year. The system I propose for Olympic lifting came from the former Soviet Union training that also covered the Bulgarian system. It must be noted that many of the ideas of I.P. Zhekov were utilized in the Bulgarian system. Many of the Soviet's top sport scientists such as Felix Meerson, N.A. Bernstein, and notables like R.A. Roman, V.V. Verkhoshansky, A.S. Medvedyev, and V.I. Zatsiorsky, have helped the author develop the strongest power team in the world, as well as the greatest male and female lifters of all time. Now I want to enlighten the American weightlifting world to what should be rightfully theirs. With the Westside conjugate system that blends the classical lifts, special exercises, volume and intensity, GPP, and restoration, this can happen.

Coaching

I have been misunderstood by many when I say America does not have good weightlifting coaches. Yes, they can teach technique, but there is much more to weightlifting success. Weightlifting has weight classes, why? Because larger men and women are stronger. The larger the weight classes the larger the records. What does this mean? Strength is very important. Now, back to the coach …

It seems today's coaches are fairly knowledgeable about technique, but when it comes to special strength exercises, the knowledge is poor at best. They demonstrate this lack of knowledge by not doing several special large exercises like pulls and special squats and small special exercises, mostly due to nonexistent equipment. The author hopes to resolve this so the lifters can once again step onto an Olympic stage. For years, the Olympic lifting community has done the same thing over and over, with the same results. Doing the same thing and expecting different results is Albert Einstein's definition of insanity. You must have an open mind—change is the hardest thing to do. But you must change if you want to save American weightlifting.

Training Methods

There are three scientifically proven methods of strength training. The Westside system uses all three inside the weekly plans.

MAXIMAL EFFORT METHOD

The first method is the greatest for raising absolute strength, it is called the Maximal Effort Method. While American weightlifters very seldom use this method, they will each week with the Westside system.

DYNAMIC METHOD

The second method, the Dynamic Method, is for two special strengths. First is explosive strength, where multiple sets at 30 percent to 40 percent are done with one and one-half to two-minute rest intervals used for recovery. The second Dynamic Method strength uses 75 percent to 85 percent for multiple sets with one and one-half to two minute rest intervals. This builds speed strength.

SUBMAXIMAL EFFORT METHOD

The third method is repetition to near failure, also referred to as the Submaximal Effort Method. Westside uses small exercises for this method, not squatting or pulling sets, which can lead to injuries when the weakest muscle fails.

To further clarify, Westside's ME day is for breaking new records. It is not intended for the classical lifts with exception of occasionally to test your progress between contests. Instead, we use special pulls, power cleans, and snatches. Special squats include front, over the head, and most off a box. A higher box will make it possible to handle weights of which you have only dreamed. Eighty percent of the ME work will be on special exercises that are rotated each training session to avoid accommodation.

By following the conjugate system you can break new records at a 95 percent success rate. This is documented at Westside by our stat man Joe Lasko. Science tells us if you handle an exercise at 90 percent for three weeks you will detrain, due to accommodation. But by rotating a special pull each week, accommodation is entirely eliminated. The author has used this system for 44 years and has found the same results D.R. Verkhoshansky found while doing his experiments at the famous Dynamo Club in 1972. They used 20 to 45 exercises and after the experiment the 70 highly ranked Olympic lifters wanted more. With up to 100 workout variations (according to Ben Tabachnik, PhD, the inventor of the speed chute), there are many special squats and pulls to experiment with to find the dozen or so to rotate your way to new totals.

When you know the most common errors in the clean and snatch, you will find that many times a weak muscle can be the case for faulty technique. When there is an absence of weak links in the body, the reliability of the lifter's success is greatly increased when you use a ratio of 80 percent special barbell exercises, as well as small special exercises. It is imperative when using the conjugate system with the barbell for pulling or squatting to establish new weight records. They must be very close in coordination structure to the classical lifts. Just as important, the bar speed must be close to the classical lift you are training for. It is possible to do more lifts in special barbell exercises than the classical lifts. You will see that the special barbell exercises will play a large role in your success.

Technique Errors

Let's look at the most common errors of highly skilled Olympic lifters in the snatch and clean and jerk and how to correct them with special exercises. In the book *Managing the Training of Weightlifters* by N.P. Laputin and V.G. Oleshko, they state that 64 percent of misses in the snatch is misdirection of the barbell, meaning the bar falls forward or backward. This is the most common error. A stronger torso can help stabilize the torso to save the lift. An Olympic lifter must have a strong back and abdominal muscles. Exercises for the spinal erectors:

- Back raise
- 45-degree back raise
- Reverse Hypers
- Goodmornings

The extension work must be heavy and high volume. Note reverse hypers should be four to one of your squat volume. Example: a 500-pound squat volume is 6,000 pounds, a hyper 24,000 pounds. The

Goodmornings are trained at roughly 70 percent of your clean for six to 10 reps per set.

For the Abs:
- Leg raises (standing or bent leg)
- Sit-ups (straight leg or bent leg, can be done on an incline)
- Zercher squats
- Wide-legged sit-ups
- Side bends
- Side presses
- Barbell twists

For GPP:
- Walking in the pool with ankle weights

This is GPP that contributes to the larger weightlifter. (Note: One must work on shoulder flexibility.)

The second most common error in the snatch, accounting for 27 percent of misses, is incomplete extension of the torso and lacking explosion. Remedies include:
- Back extensions
- 45-degree back extension
- Reverse hypers held statically
- High pulls wide and close grip
- Shrugs

The two most common errors comprise 91 percent of all failures. It is important to know why you fail.

Now, let's look at the clean and jerk.

Distortion in the jerk trajectory is most common of all errors. Again, build the torso.

The second most common error is not using the full potential of the legs and a close third is the inability to recover from the squat. This is simple: make the squat stronger. There is much to learn when building a squat. You must use a variety of special squats and exercises. When building the front squat you must use stances you don't normally use such as very wide box squats on a low box, concentric squats off a very low box, and very high pins. The high pin squats or high box squats will give new stimulus to overload the hips, lower back, upper back, and hamstrings. It is important to use a variety of special bars.

(Note: Bodybuilders and powerlifters have invented many bars over the last 40 years and have made continuous progress, while the Olympic lifter uses one bar for only three styles of squat and have virtually no progress. I hope this shows why one must use the conjugate system of rotating all types of stimulus to overcome plateaus including perfecting technique. By introducing special exercises instead of working with light weights for technique when, after all, it is the most heavy weights you need to improve.)

A Different Future

This book is intended to raise results in training as well as meets. Technique is taught at an easy age of nine to 11-years-old and being constantly monitored throughout your training. But if one develops a muscle imbalance, two things will happen: one—injuries; and two—progress stops. Valeriy Borzov and his coach Valentin Belize said that to run faster you must train 90 percent to 100 percent of your maximum. Even by the 1960's, Arkady Vorobyev, the head weightlifting coach of the national weightlifting team, came to the same conclusion. The barbell must approach close to max in the classical lift and constantly break records in special pulls and squats in training. By rotating the bar exercises, as well as small special exercises that help contribute to raising the pulls and squats, you will get better results. As you can see in track, Olympic lifting, or powerlifting, training is training.

Chapter 2 - Squats and Special Exercises

Chapter 2: Squats and Special Exercises

The weightlifter must improve the squat (back, overhead, and front). Many times, a weightlifter will visit Westside with a 360-pound clean and when asked about his front squat, he replies 370 pounds. This is typical but not advisable. The odds are not good to clean an all-time record, then front squat an all-time record and many times a jerk record as well. While it is advised to hold the squat at a percent over your clean, this thinking can hold back your progress. Light-weight men and women must have very strong legs to counteract errors in technique due to the lesser mass of their heavier counterparts. When an athletically built lifter's squat goes up, so should his pulls. Thinner lifters are better designed to pull weights, but find squatting a difficult task due to bad leverages.

So how do you raise the Olympic style squatting? Simple: by not doing them. Yes, that means following the Conjugate Method (remember when you constantly do the same thing over and over you will slow or stop progress through the law of accommodation). You will hear this over and over.

Let's Look At a Different Method

FIRST—BOX SQUATS

Before you reject box squatting, consider the action of my good friend Eskil Thomasson from Sweden who trained at Westside for 10 years. While visiting back in Europe, he made a stop at the Polish weightlifting facility and found a 1950 weightlifting manual. It showed box squatting. I believe throwers that came to America to visit the original Westside Barbell in Culver City, California, back in the 70's introduced box squatting to them.

But why box squat? Box squatting can build the exact muscles that regular squatting does not. You can squat wider and lower on a box, than without a box. The box makes it possible to relax some of the muscles while other muscles are held static. Static can be overcome by dynamic. This is scientifically proven to be two of the greatest methods of strength training. This procedure will build the glutes, as well as the hips, to the max.

With Olympic style squatting, the glutes are pulled forward toward the ankles. This lessens the work of the glutes and hamstrings. The box squat does the opposite. It pushes the glutes out to the rear and the knees are pushed outward as well to develop the inner legs. The box is built to sit on, rock back loading the hips then concentrically raise straight up. The torso is inclined to some extent simulating the position while pulling. One can full squat 15 percent more on the average than their box squat at the same height.

As a bonus, all styles of Olympic squatting may be used—back, front, and overhead on a variety of heights. For some reason there is very little max effort work by the American weightlifters by using a high box squat to do the three varieties of squat with weights that you have never handled before. Having had many Olympic lifters visit Westside and sitting on a low box was almost impossible without falling the last few inches. They possess little eccentric strength. I noticed the same thing when catching a power clean well above parallel only to fall into a full squat. Has no one noticed this and realized there is a problem?

There must be several special exercises to raise the ability to increase the squat. Let's look at one such exercise.

BELT SQUATS

The former Soviet lifters called them leg squats and they served several purposes. One, they allowed one to train the legs while resting an overtrained or injured back. They also help repair pelvic tilt, but also overloaded the legs. They did them just like Westside with a belt around the waist with weight suspended by a chain through plates while standing on two boxes and squatting down between them.

A second, and far more superior, method is a Westside belt squat machine. This is a cable machine with a belt around the waist. This machine allows one to regular squat as well as box squat. Two other methods are to do static squat holds. This one exercise was a major reason Josh Conley pushed his deadlift from 700 pounds to 900 pounds officially in 16 months. The weights used are estimated to be from 1,500 pounds to 2,000 pounds plus.

Westside also duplicates an old Olympic lifting exercise. While doing a one-quarter squat in the belt squat machine, Westside will do high pulls or cleans. By separating the lower body from the upper body acceleration, one will build incredible strength in the hips and legs.

Other special squats that must be included in your program are power rack, or chain squats. These are concentric style and you must lower yourself under the bar and squat from a dead stop. Front, back, and overhead squats must be used. Also, perfect form must be used on all squats all the time. Remember to switch special squat bars each week on ME day and every three-week pendulum wave on a speed strength day 72 hours later.

POWER RACK SQUATS—SHOCK METHODS

Plyometrics always come to mind when shock methods are discussed, but there are several shock methods that provide intense stimulation to force the athlete to his or her highest level of training adaptation. One shock method is supramaximal lifts.

With the use of a power rack, one can do one-quarter and half squats that far exceed the best regular squat possible. Squat concentrically off pins or do high box squats with 100 pounds or more than your best squat. This will cause the body to function at a level never before experienced.

The power rack with its safety pins makes it possible and safe to do maximal eccentrics. Olympic lifters drop down very fast in most cases. This makes it necessary to do eccentrics on occasion. The power rack can be used to spot the lifter with its safety pins while doing contrast method training with weight releasers or strong rubber bands. All squats can be performed—front, back, and overhead. The power rack is a must-use tool for the Olympic lifter. Rack pulls at a variety of pin heights for overloads and, of course, isometric training against pins, and the Hoffman method where you pull off a lower pin to a higher pin and hold for three to five seconds. Many times rack work is referred to as restricted range maximums.

NOTE: STRENGTH POTENTIAL

There is a great need for power rack training with weights far above the classical lifts limits. Olympic lifters need to slow down many of their lifts. While 50 percent of training should fall between 75 percent and 85 percent for speed strength. But as we know, when weights grow heavier they also slow down. Strength is measured in velocities, explosive strength in fast velocity, speed strength in intermediate velocity, and strength speed in slow velocity. While speed strength is 75 percent to 85 percent of a one-rep max, one rep maxes will comprise a large load of the training. It builds speed strength and the percentages are good for perfecting technique. Weight at 90 percent and above must be trained roughly 25 percent of the time. During a competition cycle at least 50 percent of the training will be special pulls, squats, and jerks with the pull at 95 percent to 100 percent. The heavy weight will be on ME day. I recommend breaking the special pulls, squats, and jerks by 2.5 kg. This makes it fun and forces the body to use more in muscle units as you must lift large weights in training. Your body will adapt only to the loads placed upon it. Never psych in training because it is only a training max. Save high emotions for a contest max.

Keep the heavy pull to no more than three with the third being a small PR. Refer to the 2.5 record as the plan. You plan on breaking a record—be satisfied and move on or coordination can be ill affected. Remember, the large volume of 80 percent should be on small special exercises for the development of the pulls, squats, and jerk. The classical lifts are 20 percent.

WHY!

In America the rule of three does not exist—meaning there is no base work. Back raises and glute/hams will build a larger pull and squat. So why drop them close to the contest when they account for your early success?

Special Exercises

SMALL SPECIAL EXERCISES

I started out Olympic lifting at 14-years-old, and I could squat 410 at 148 pounds at that time. I continued to do the same-style training and at 18-years-old my squat was the same. I was drafted at 18-years-old and upon entering the Army I read Muscle Power Builder and an article about boxing by the original Westside in Culver City, California. They suggested not only box squatting but Goodmornings, back raises, and an assortment of small special exercises. At the 1971 Jr. Nationals, my squat was 565 pounds at a bodyweight of 170 pounds. It was the conjugate system—but what made my regular squat go up was not squatting. Using a series of exercises for the low and upper back plus hamstrings, Olympic lifts, even calves was the reason the squat moved up. I also squatted 630 pounds and deadlifted 670 pounds at 180 pounds.

LARGE SPECIAL EXERCISES

Many Soviet training manuals show a list of 100 fundamental exercises for weightlifting. Ben Tabachnik Ph.D. talks about such a list in Soviet Training and Recovery Methods written by Rick Brunner and Ben Tabachnik. The list appeared in Supertraining by Dr. Mel Siff.

For some reason many coaches only want to practice six or seven lifts, this leads to accommodation, meaning a decrease in progress. Of course one cannot incorporate 100 special barbell exercises into a short program. But you must experiment and find sets of exercises to do in a workout and learn to rotate a group into a three-week wave on speed strength day. Remember speed strength is trained at 75 percent to 85 percent When using a special barbell exercise on ME day, work up to a small personal record (meaning 2.5 kg to 5 kg), then turn to a second special barbell exercise and quickly work up to a second small PR for the second exercise of the day (again, a small PR—2.5 kg to 5 kg) and move on. Do the small special exercises for the legs or back.

Example:
- Power snatch bar at below knees
- Power snatch bar above knees
- Overhead squat with snatch grip

- Glute ham raises, reverse hypers, back raises, and jumps

This is ME day.

With 100 more exercises to make many revolving workouts, pick one that works for you and that produces progress. You must have a large arsenal of special bars to avoid accommodation. Besides special bars, rubber bands of at least three strengths must be employed into your training.

THE KEY

Remember, a ratio of 20 percent barbell training and 80 percent special exercises must make up 100 percent of your training to correct lifting form. If you pull your knees inward while recovering from a heavy squat, why do you think more squats will fix the problem? It won't, of course. If you can't hold the lockout in your jerk or snatch do you really think it will correct itself? No, you must at the very least do elbow extensions.

Westside breaks everything down to the smallest denominator. First, you must be able to recover from the high-volume training. This requires General Physical Preparedness (GPP). A high work capacity is a must, and this is why a person must have good leverages—or body proportions—to excel in lifting. For GPP you can mix strong man training such as yoke, farmers walks, sled pulling of all types, or swimming/riding a bike. These will help restore your body. I hear all the time that lifters are overtrained. This is more likely to be out of shape. If you follow the math shown in our programming it is impossible to become overtrained.

SMALL SPECIAL EXERCISE EXAMPLES

I have mentioned the value of small exercises. Take a look at Josh Conley, a 900-pound deadlifter. He does 50,000 pounds of explosive leg presses and 50,000 pounds of reverse hypers pre workout twice a week, plus inverse hamstring curls and an undetermined amount of static holds in a belt squat machine, adding up to a minimum of 150,000 pounds of work on an individual muscle group. Josh's squat tonnage one week is 13,200 pounds— this is correct for a 1,100-pound squat. On speed strength day and max effort day, the squat, pull, or Goodmorning volume is at least 40 percent of speed strength. The small special exercises are of very high volume.

For the Back:
- Light Goodmorning
- Back raise
- 45-degree back raise
- Reverse hyper
- Upright rows
- Bent over rows
- One arm snatch
- One arm deadlift
- Pull ups/ chin ups
- Straight leg deadlift

For the Legs:
- Glute ham raise
- Inverse curls
- Leg curls of all types
- Leg press
- Jumps
- Lunges
- One-legged squats
- Belt squats
- Static squats
- Depth jumps

General work for the back and legs:
- Sled pulling
- Wheel barrow
- Yoke
- Walking with weight vest
- Farmer carry

While this represents a small list, use three or four per workout after the main barbell exercises.

Chapter 3: Speed Strength Training

Chapter 3: Speed Strength Training

Weightlifting is a speed strength sport according to A.D Ermakov and N.S Atanasov. Data in 1975 analyzed distributions of training loads. In 780 cases, their highest skilled weightlifters used 75 percent to 85 percent effort 50 percent of the time. Knowing this, I plan speed strength day doing a three-week pendulum wave with 75 percent to 85 percent effort. This wave is repeated week-in and week-out throughout the yearly plan. How do we avoid accommodation? Each week we change something. Here is a small example:

POWER SNATCH FROM THE FLOOR:

Week 1: 75% 6x2 reps

Week 2: 80% 6x2 reps

Week 3: 85% 5x2 reps

POWER SNATCH FROM BELOW THE KNEE:

Week 4: 75% 6x2 reps

Week 5: 80% 6x2 reps

Week 6: 85% 5x2 reps

SNATCH WITH BAR BELOW THE KNEE (SQUAT STYLE):

Week 7: 75% 6x2 reps

Week 8: 80% 6x2 reps

Week 9: 85% 5x2 reps

SNATCH WITH BAR ABOVE THE KNEE (SQUAT STYLE):

Week 10: 75% 6x2

Week 11: 80% 6x2

Week 12: 85% 5x2

In the same workout you will perform 12 lifts in the clean and jerk of some variation. Again, I follow the fine work of A.S Prilepin's 1974 research on the number of lifts, not only as a set, but also a workout. This changed Westside in 1982. I concentrate on more strength than speed. The Americans look fine with light weight, but cannot do world-class weights. When your coach says you don't need to be strong to lift big weights, ask him why there are weight classes. If strength does not play a role, why do you have weight classes or why don't women lift what their male counterparts lift? It is a lack of strength and power.

You will find many speed strength programs in Chapter 8: Speed Strength and Max Effort Workouts. The 75 percent to 85 percent weights will promote good technique while building high volume to calculate how much max effort volume three days later. Plus, regulate the high volume of small special exercises after the classical lifts. Remember that 80 percent of your training will be small special exercises for the back, legs, and torso.

Chapter 4: Methods

Chapter 4: Methods

We know that the majority of regular training must be at 75 percent to 85 percent, while the Max Effort Method is the most effective for improving both intramuscular and intermuscular coordination. It is the method that makes it possible to lift the largest weights possible.

So let's concentrate on both of the two methods when lifting. The Dynamic Method is used when lifting submaximal weights with maximal speed (F= MA). This builds and improves the rate of force development and explosive strength. Concentrate on weights at 75 percent to 85 percent for the speed strength waves and max weights based off the most you are able to do on that particular day. Always try for an all-time record. At Westside, Joe Lasko the statistician, records 90 percent to 95 percent success rate for the 20 or so members. Our speed strength average mean weight is 80 percent for the high volume day, and mostly 100 percent plus on ME day.

Nain Suleymanoglu is one of – if not the greatest – Olympic weightlifter of all time. His average intensity was 87 percent. The max effort training at Westside is a combination of the percent success rate for breaking all-time records on special barbell exercises. The great V. Alexeyev used the very same style of wave periodization relayed to me by Dr. Mel Siff of Supertraining fame. He also used many special exercises of his own choice like back raises and inverse curls, which were so important that they actually kept stats. They must have played a great role in his training success leading up to his all-time world records.

Westside is a powerlifting dynasty, breaking upwards of 140 world records and only all-time lifts are counted. The training is based on Olympic lifting and track and field—there are no regular squats, only box squats. Train the bench for explosive power, meaning 40 percent of a one rep max (1RM) and zero deadlifts, yet we have two 900-pound deadlifters using this system. IT WILL WORK FOR WHOM IT WAS INTENDED FOR, the weightlifter.

1. Keep notes on what wave was the most effective.
2. Know what did not work – don't make the same mistakes.
3. What should be added?
4. What helped speed strength and strength speed?
5. How often should the best exercises be used in a monthly or yearly plan?
6. What works best before a meet?

Prilepin's study suggests a minimum, a maximum, and an optimal number of reps per set as well as the number of lifts per workout. By using the number of lifts per workout multiplied by the percent converted to poundage to reach a total volume. We do this for you. First look at the squat programs and you will see how the volume is calculated. When you research Prilepin's data you will see 18 lifts optimal at 70 percent and 15 lifts optimal at 80 percent weight. After the power or classical lifts are done, you must squat. The power or classical lifts should be done every two minutes and the rest for squatting should be the same. This makes training dense, and allows a lot of time to do special exercises.

Special exercises play a large role in our system. At least 80 percent of the training is special exercises for the legs, back, and torso. Squatting and pulling can get you just so far. One must concentrate on making a larger squat. After you stop making progress, all the squatting in the world will not help. This could be due to the lack of glutes and hamstrings. The answer is calf ham/glute raises or reverse hypers along with inverse leg curls. If your back is not strong enough to match your leg strength, we do a great deal of belt squats and static holds in the belt squat machine. The machines or exercises I have just mentioned are far more important than bumper plates.

If your pulls have come to a halt, you need back raises: 45-degree back raises, upright rows, bent over rows, many forms of sled walking, even grip work can hold back a record clean or snatch. This sounds like GPP (general physical preparedness), but is completely necessary. Let's look at the three methods of training you must do and why.

Maximal Effort Method

This method is superior to all others for breaking records in weightlifting. It is best for improving intra-muscular and intermuscular coordination. Remember the CNS (Central Nervous System) and muscles adapt only to the loads placed on them. Work up to a 1RM for a small record and move on. A squat and a pull record can be broken in a single workout, or two pulls. An example would be pull from below the knee and pull from above the knee. The volume must be kept low with the barbell, leaving the high volume to small special exercises. Rotate to new exercises each week as well. When using the same exercises for three weeks at 90 percent or above you will go backwards. The Maximal Effort Method (ME) system eliminated this, plus other staleness syndrome.

Symptoms are:
- High blood pressure
- Tiredness
- Unable to wake in morning easily
- And so forth.

ME is to be done once a week. For pulls and squats, a second ME day can be used for pressing and jerks. Don't work up to a heavy weight. It is much better and completely possible to do an all-time record mostly in special pulls and squats. This is exactly how you break all-time records in the power clean, power snatch, and the classical lifts. Westside has a 95 percent success rate, and so will you. This explanation may not be the most scientific, but you can refer to Science and Practice of Strength Training by V.M Zatsiorsky (second edition 2006).

Advanced lifters can do a second ME workout on a second movement. Jerk from stands concentric squat, a version of the overhead squat, a snatch or clean pull, with 20 minutes rest between ME lifts.

MAX EFFORT WORKOUTS

Below is a list of max effort workouts. They consist of special pulls, squats, jerks, and presses.
- Power snatch with overhead squat
- Snatch from boxes with overhead squat
- Push press plus jerk off a rack
- Clean pull with shrugs
- Snatch from hang
- Front squat plus push press
- Clean pull to shoulders plus front squat
- Clean pull with straight legs
- Power clean plus front squat
- Power clean standing on a 2" box

- Back squat plus jerk behind the head
- Push press wide grip
- Box squat high box
- Box squat low box
- Box squat low box front squat
- Box squat off low pin
- Overhead squat off pin
- Squat plus goodmorning
- Incline press
- Belt squat max weight

This is a small list of special exercises to break records on ME day. Feel free to change stances from very close to very wide. The grip can change for the jerk, press, and snatch from very wide to very close. Don't forget isometrics as well. Isometrics are very valuable for not only the lifters, but the coach. By holding a position for three to six seconds, a coach can watch and easily analyze the technique of the lifter at any point of the lift.

REACHING THE TOP

To reach the top of weightlifting, you must constantly raise volume while it is based off your max lifts by using the correct percentage. For instance, for speed strength day the weights will range from 75 percent to 85 percent in a three-week wave. These percentages are established from the data of A.D Ermakov and N.S Atanasov's 1975 study with 780 highly skilled weightlifters. Fifty percent of their training consisted of weights between 75 percent and 85 percent. The number of lifts per workout is established from A.S Prilepin's work in 1974.

Dynamic Effort Method

While Max Effort Method is best for increasing max strength, it is impossible to only use max effort training. Knowing that a severe workout can be done every 72 hours and realizing it was impossible to recover from only max effort workouts, Westside introduced a Dynamic Method workout in its place. It serves two purposes—one is to increase a fast rate of force development. It was not intended to raise maximal strength. It is impossible to attain Fmm in fast movements against intermediate resistance. We as powerlifters had to find a way to increase the rate of force development and explosive strength that was a trait of weightlifters. It is simple: "a powerlifter needs to move weights faster, and a weightlifter needs to move weights slower." Yes slower! As weights grow heavier, the bar slows down, and here is where the weightlifter fails. This is why weightlifters must use max effort.

Now, the second reason why the Dynamic Method must be utilized is to perfect lifting form in the classical lifts, with optimal weights 75 percent to 85 percent for speed strength. The average weight lifted during the dynamic workout is 80 percent in a three-week wave. By following the pre-calibrated percentages and using correct rest intervals—roughly two minutes—the well prepared athlete will recover.

Many workouts can be used for the Dynamic Method by starting the barbell at the floor or on a two-inch box, below the knee, at the knee, and above the knee. By rotating every three-week wave you will avoid accommodation. Once more: a one-week wave for max effort, three-week wave for speed strength, the Dynamic Method, and one for strength speed and the Max Effort Method.

Submaximal and Repeated Effort Method

These methods are intended to build muscle mass. Only a few barbell exercises are used: the Good-morning (70 percent, three to six reps) and Dimel deadlifts (20 reps at 30 percent), for example. Our theory is very high reps—up to 30 per set (such as reverse hypers or leg presses)—are to build muscle where we want it. Back raises, glute/ham raises and inverse hamstring curls are examples. The author watched Waldemar Baszanowski do sets of five reps in the back raise with 225 pounds at 148-pound bodyweight for the 1970 world championships.

Inside page 79 of the *Science and Practice of Strength Training* second edition it shows data from V Alexeev, the 1972 and 1976 Olympic champion, doing inverse curls for the back and hamstrings. This tells the author it was of great importance to him to chart his work and progress. Again, your total volume should be about 80 percent for special exercises. We show many special exercises including belt squats of many types plus reverse hypers, which both work as restoration and at the same time build great strength.

Look at *Managing the Training of Weightlifters* by N.P Laputin and V.G Oleshko to clarify much of what I have discussed.

Chapter 5: Increasing Explosive Strength and Reactive Method Through Plyometrics

Chapter 5: Increasing Explosive Strength and Reactive Method Through Plyometrics

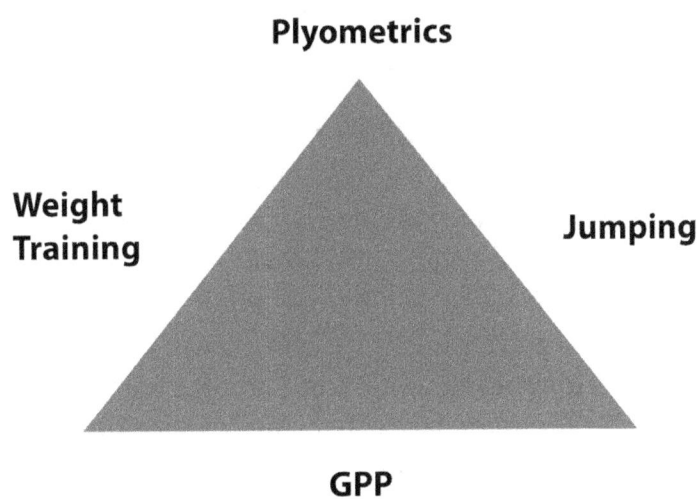

Shock training or plyometrics is developed by a sudden stretch preceding any voluntary effort. Plyometrics is used to increase explosive strength and reactive method. Kinetic Energy and not heavy weights must be used. Two common means are depth jumps and med ball rebounding.

The first thoughts on this topic by Dr. Verkhoshansky, the father of plyometrics, came by observing triple jumpers and how powerful the jumps were after each landing. He knew that the powerful jumps came after the athletes' falling body reacted to the impact of the contact to the ground. This made Verkhoshansky aware of the stretch-shortening action by the use of kinetic energy. Some believe that plyometrics are dangerous. They can be without the proper knowledge of general weight and jump training before engaging in depth jumps. While depth jumps build explosive strength, they also build absolute strength by using different heights to achieve a certain goal. How many drops are done in one workout for the intermediate or advanced? You will note that Olympic lifting is never mentioned when the goal is developing explosive power or strength. Why is that?

Strength is not measured in heavy or light weights. What is a heavy 300-pound squat for a female sprinter would be light for a world-class shot putter. So how can one weight be heavy and light? It can't, but rather fast or slow. Strength is measured in velocities.

Explosive = fast velocity

Speed Strength = intermediate velocity

Strength Speed = low velocity

Isometric = zero velocity

This is explained on pg. 150 in Supertraining, sixth edition, 2003.

Are Depth Jumps and Bounding Safe?

Depth jumps and bounding are just as safe as running, jumping or many other ballistic sport activities. What makes them unsafe is a lack of a complete training system. Before the subject of plyometric training, we must first prescribe sound weight training and jump training. Let's look at the three proven methods of weight training.

1. THE DYNAMIC METHOD

This method improves the rate of force development and speed and explosive strength. It is of no use to build maximal strength, but certainly had a lot to do with its development. As your max's go up are you able to maintain the same bar speed at sub maximal weights? Fifty percent of speed strength should be at 50 percent to 60 percent of a one rep max with 25 percent band tension at the lockout. Training roughly at 0.8 to 0.9 m/s on average. This is mechanical power.

2. MAXIMAL EFFORT METHOD

This is the greatest method of strength training for improving both intermuscular and intramuscular coordination, as your body only adapts to the load placed upon it. Then work up after a warm-up to single attempts until setting a new record. Stop for the day and seven days later switch a special barbell exercise and max-out once more. This is low volume, highest intensity training followed by three to four small special exercises.

The Maximal Effort Method uses slow velocity while the Dynamic Method uses intermediate velocity. The two methods make it possible to absorb the harsh training plyometric demands of the athlete. Explosive strength is trained at fast velocity. It is trained by a variety of special exercises with and without weights or other resistance.

3. THE REPETITION METHOD

This method should not be done in the classical lift but in small exercises, especially for the posterior chain. Note: the posterior chain is talked about all the time, but I see athletes constantly lacking strength in that area. Eighty percent of Westside training is small special exercises, while only 20 percent is classical.

Basic Jump Program

A group of jumping exercises first came from dance and were later incorporated into weight lifting and track and field. Examples are: Seated press on the floor, where you can consider kneeling squats front and back, jumping on the feet; Power clean off knee's onto feet; power snatch off knees onto feet; and power clean or snatch off knees into a split style. Add weights when possible while keeping records on each type of jump.

Next, consider box jumping with weights, use kettlebells, weight vests, ankle weights, and combos of all types. Keep records of every type, always rotating each jump session to avoid accommodation. Forty jumps are recommended per workout for the very strong or at least advanced athlete 18 years and older. To round out the athlete's preparatory phase, power walk with sleds. This will build strong jumping and running muscles as well as thicker ligaments and tendons including the feet, where many career ending or at least season-ending injuries occur. Westside DVD's cover all the above information about the volume and intensity. The coach and athlete must learn to train smarter not harder. Like ACDC said "it's a long road if you want to reach the top." Now you are ready for plyometric training. Like all the shock methods can be taxing, plyometrics are no different. So before depth jumps let's look at several types of bounding with ground contact under 0.2 of a second.

1. Single take-off jumps on stairs
2. Leg to leg jumps: single, triple, 5's and 10's
3. Double leg jumps over five to 10 or 15 low hurdles
4. Double leg jumps over high hurdles of 40" to 42"
5. Slow bounds with submaximal effort in a controlled style

6. Frog jumps

7. Three jumps off left foot then three jumps off right foot

8. 20/40/60 meter leg-to-leg bounds with light resistance 10-20-30 pounds with Bulgarian bag

9. Standing long jumps (keep records)

10. Standing long jumps with Kettlebells, release before landing

The above jumps should be done after weight lifting dynamic or max effort with a 30-minute rest from the barbell lifts.

EXPLOSIVE WEIGHT JUMPS

Do a single to a triple with 30 percent of a one rep max or 10 to 15 percent of a one rep max with Kettlebells or Bulgarian bags for 10 to 20 reps. Stop when fatigue sets in. While Dr. Verkhoshansky uses contrast training with a heavy barbell for one to two reps at 90 percent, immediately followed by 30 percent barbell jumps, Westside does it differently. We use band resistance by the barbell for an over speed eccentric phase to produce more kinetic energy for reversible strength, and the bands give accommodation to eliminate bar deceleration.

DEPTH JUMPS

First, what is the goal? Explosive power or absolute strength?

The height of the drop will determine the outcome. Thirty-six-inch drops and lower will build explosive power. Drop jumps of 45 inches and higher will build absolute strength, but can be very dangerous. They are never for beginners or large, over 125 kg, athletes. The time of the fall until ground contact will determine the amortization phase or shock absorption phase, which must be 0.2 of a second or faster to be considered a plyometric action. When falling from a greater height, the shock absorption phase will be longer, mainly training a strong isometric contraction in the leg muscles. Do four sets of 10 drops for the advanced and three sets of eight drops for well trained. Remember the amortization phase is most important. In the beginning, drop off a low box 12-16-20 inches. The coach must analyze the time spent on the ground. Just like sprinting, the less ground contact, the better.

DEPTH DROPS VS. DEPTH JUMPS

Depth drops will provide the ability to absorb the shock of the fall, but are not as effective due to not using an energetic take off to develop reactive ability. Like many things, there are many varieties of depth jumps, but like box squats, there is only one correct method.

Note: I am always amazed that great sport scientist like Dr. Verkhoshansky spent years perfecting the perfect technique in a proven exercise, only to have un-experienced coaches use their own ideas that lead to less than favorable results, then assume the inventor was wrong in his assumption of its value. So, to reduce the risk of injuries and to make depth jumps as valuable to the athlete as possible. I will describe Dr. Verkhoshansky's method for performing the exercise.

Dr. Verkhoshansky's Depth Jump Method

The athlete must start with arms behind the back. Then, step off a pre-determined height box with one leg stepping forward at the start of the fall. Now bring the other leg forward to even. After stepping off the box the legs must be straight. Remember do not jump but fall from the box forward, straight down to the landing surface.

HOW TO LAND

The athlete must land on both legs simultaneously on the balls of the feet, then back on the heels. Now, upon landing be flexible to cushion the surface contact before the takeoff.

THE TAKEOFF PHASE

The athlete now must jump as high as possible. One can set a vertical jump tester to establish the height to reach. Try new records and keep an account from different height drops. I prefer to drop jump from a pre-determined box and jump upward on the second box. This is somewhat less taxing because your velocity is near zero upon landing on an elevated box. When jumping upward to touch a new height you now must once again do a safe landing to try to land as easy as possible on the balls of both feet with a flexible surface (rubber mats or foam).

Note: Because depth jumps can alter the work load to such an extent you must limit some squatting and pulling exercises during depth jump training.

WESTSIDE USE OF DEPTH JUMPS

Westside uses the recommendations of Dr. Verkhoshansky: four sets of 10 jumps two times a week. Average drop height is 30 inches. Three sets of eight jumps for not so advanced, meaning well trained and very strong. Our weight jumps use the same loading. Remember, you must be physically prepared to do depth jumps. Weight training for max strength, speed strength and explosive through jumping up onto boxes. A large base for GPP is sled work, wheel barrow push and 80 percent of the training must be small special exercises.

Recommended Reading

Supertraining by Mel Siff; *Science and Practice of Strength Training* by V. M Zatsiorsky; *Special Strength Training Manual for Coaches* by Y. Verkhoshansky; *Fundamentals of Special Strength Training in Sports* by Y.V. Verkhoshansky; *Explosive Power and Jumping Ability* by T. Starzynski and H. Sozanski PHD; Lifts DVD by Natalia Verkhoshansky

Chapter 6: Periodization—Division Into Training Periods

Chapter 6: Periodization—Division Into Training Periods

I knew Western periodization was a dead-end as early as 1973, which was the year I broke my back for the first time, but I knew no other way. In 1981 after breaking my L5 the second time, I had to find a better way. I would be strong in one lift, but not the other two. It would be a different lift that would go up while some other lifts were unmanageable. Ricky Crain, a great lifter, would call me with the same story. Dave Waddington, the first 1,000-pound squatter was in my living room and asked how to fix the same problem Ricky and I had. I told him to call me when he found the answer.

So back to 1981, I was desperate. I made a call to Bud Charniga to buy some Soviet books on training. He said, "Lou, you know these are like text books written by their Sports scientists on very intricate matters on training." I told Bud that is exactly what I needed because the Western gradual overload system led me down a dead-end road. It is more of a de-training system than anything else. But, enough talking about the past.

Three-Week Speed Strength Waves

I looked at the models of Matveyev, his wave system, and the wave-like concentration of loading for five to eight weeks at a time by Verkhoshansky. I then looked at the pendulum approach by Arosiev, which is used for alternating special strength preparation such as speed strength, explosive strength, strength speed and even strength endurance. I also looked at Tudor O. Bompa, Ph.D., and his findings. It was interesting to me how effective the system was that made Naim Suleymanoglu the great Bulgarian weightlifter. I realized the system was for a model athlete or someone of perfect proportion for his sport. It was based on the hypothesis of Felix Meerson (Plasticeskoe Obezpecenie Organizma, 1967) and Hiden's findings from 1960-1964.

Which one was the best, or was there a best? These were, after all, very intelligent men, to say the least. I had found before that, however, I did not like a long-term plan. I discovered in my training and my training plateaus that after going upward for three weeks, I would regress almost every time. I like the wave system of training by Matveyev and Verkhoshansky, but Vorobyev's (1978) wave plan was a little less restrictive, somewhat like Ermakov's work in 1974.

Dr. Siff asked me how I came up with a three-week speed strength wave. I told him I became no stronger or faster after three weeks, and he was fascinated to hear that because V. Alexez, the great Soviet SHW lifter, used the same three-week wave. On week four, he re-evaluated the training and started a new three-week wave cycle. I think I won Mel Siff over at that point.

There are some different approaches I implement, and I seldom do a regular squat or deadlift. As the meet approaches, we don't reduce special exercises, but push them to the limit to perfect form by concentrating on the weak muscle group. This is what the conjugate system does. There are three phases that are strength training: Maximal effort, Dynamic Method, and Repetition Method for hypertrophy, which are all trained simultaneously. There is built-in flexibility in a three week pendulum wave.

Volume and Intensity Zones

The first graphs concerning volume and intensity zones also show the importance of waving the volume and percentage of a one rep max again to avoid accommodation. The speed strength days show high volume and moderate to low intensity. On max effort days, the opposite will and must occur. The volume is 35 percent to 50 percent of the speed days, but as the intensities must be as high as possible, hopefully, a new all-time record will be set. Like the Bulgarian, the level of preparedness is the major factor for how much one can lift on max effort day.

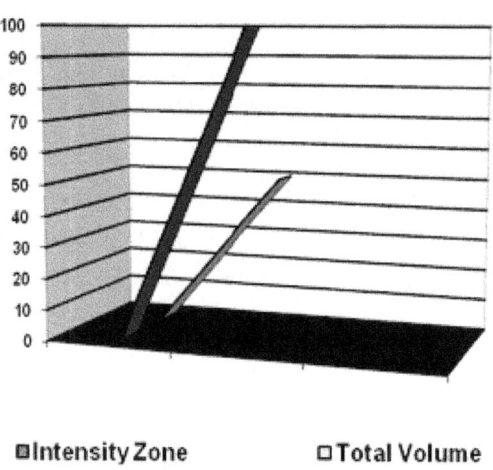

Figure 1.1. Low volume training; highest intensity possible for 100 percent and above. Limit to three lifts of 90 percent and above

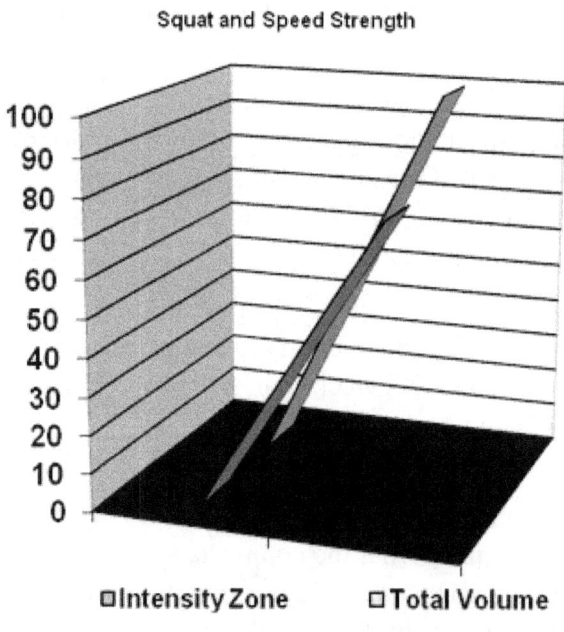

Figure 1.2. High volume training; moderate intensity zones, between 60 percent to 85 percent. Limit to 12 to 24 lifts per training session.

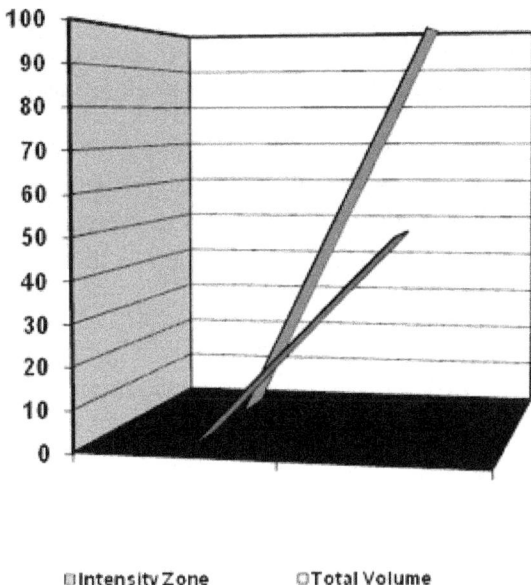

Figure 1.3. High Volume training; low to moderate intensity, between 50 percent to 60% percent. Limit 16 to 30 lifts per training session.

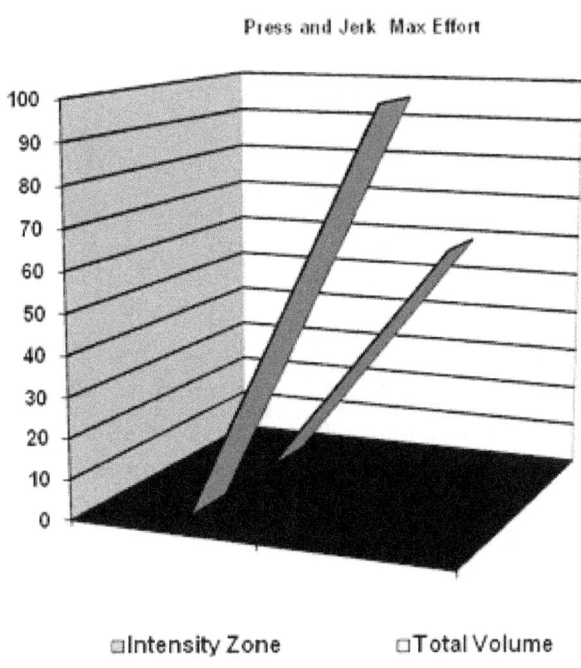

Figure 1.4. Low volume training; highest intensity possible. Limit to three lifts of 90 percent and above.

Four Direct Periods of Periodization

1. **Accumulation** – high volume training of all types to charge or build the body for speed or strength for a particular sport.

2. **Intensification** – now the athlete limits to some degree the exercises concentrating on more specific speed work or strength movements that work best for him or her.

3. **Transformation** – now the value of the previous two cycles is to test while the athlete uses exercises that are most beneficial to the competition. For lifting, the top lifter uses a circa-max or near-max weight phase with limited special exercise that contribute to his or her highest achievements. A runner's work would be very limited to the very most important speed or speed endurance work.

4. **Delayed Transformation** – here, one reduces the high intensity work and relies on rest and restoration for two to four weeks leading up to a competition. We found that 21 days is best for the heaviest training weight. We then taper down to meet time.

It is imperative to know about these phases of training. Refer to the suggested reading for more information on periodization.

THE IMPORTANCE OF OBSERVATION

During the Westside system of using a three-week wave for speed strength and explosive speed training, the wave rotates from 75 percent to 85 percent in a three-week cycle, jumping 5 percent per week. By doing this, I can evaluate the progress of the athlete all the time. This makes more sense to observe the athlete to see if he has become stronger or faster as well as other physical qualities such as quickness or where muscle mass should be added. I don't have a crystal ball, so I have no idea where the athlete's progress will be in 12 weeks or 24 weeks. The three-week wave system allows for better observation on a continuous basis. For maximal effort work each week the major barbell exercises are changed.

ELIMINATING ACCOMMODATION

Soviet sports scientists found after three weeks of weight training at 90 percent or more, progress stopped. This is accommodation, but it is totally eliminated by revolving the barbell exercises each week. We can max out every week throughout the year, and extreme workouts can occur every 72 hours. Our weekly plan is to speed squat on Friday with high volume of 75 percent to 85 percent intensity zone for three reps per set. On Monday it is max effort work for squatting or pulling for max singles. The intensity is 100 percent plus all an individual can do on that particular day similar to the Bulgarian system. No more than three lifts from 90 percent up to a new max. Of course, the volume is low much like the Rule of 60 percent. Speed press and jerks on Sunday. High volume and very low intensity zones range from 40 percent to 50 percent. Wednesday is max effort day, working up to a new personal record or as much as possible. Do this with single lifts not more than three lifts at 90 percent, approaching 100 percent; plus, in one week the speed work is 20 to 30 lifts while the max effort day is three lifts. It is almost a 10 to 1 ratio with speed lifts beginning the 10, and max lifts being 1.

The bulk of our system is special exercises. We do not have a system to form a model athlete, so it may take several combinations of special exercises to make one succeed. Our entire training program is built around special exercises for weight lifting, powerlifting or running and jumping. I don't concentrate on what you have, but rather what you don't have.

An NFL agent brought in a lineman and asked me what I was going to do. I told him, and he said, "Why aren't you going to run him?" I asked him this question, "He ran for four years and this is how fast he is. Why do you think two more months of running with him will make a difference?" He replied, "Good point."

Nine-Week Training Cycle

Let's look at pendulum waves with special bars. The graphs show a nine-week training cycle, consisting of three different three-week pendulum waves. The nine-week system employs three types of bars. They each have a maximum weight to calculate the percentage. All three maximums are different to avoid the mistake of accommodation or using the same volume repeatedly. The bar path will be somewhat different as well to ensure training all leg and back muscles. The bar speed by percents will be close, but the bar weight is quite different.

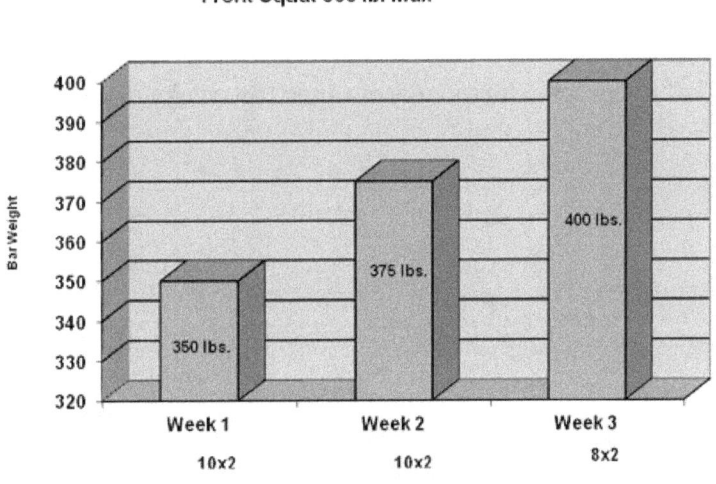

Figure 2.1. This graph shows bar weight for weeks one through three.

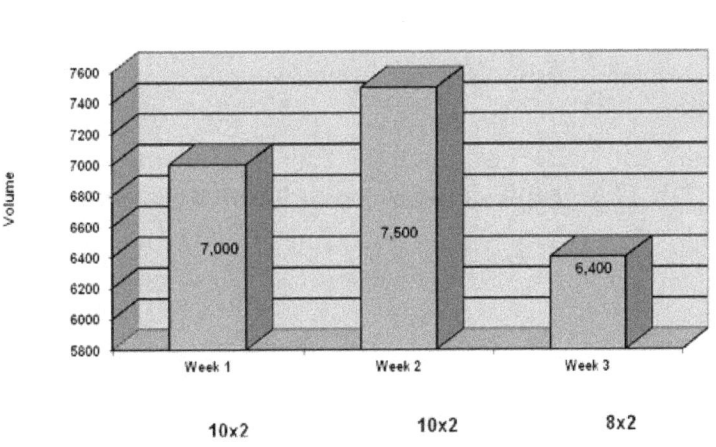

Figure 2.2. This graph shows volume for weeks one through three.

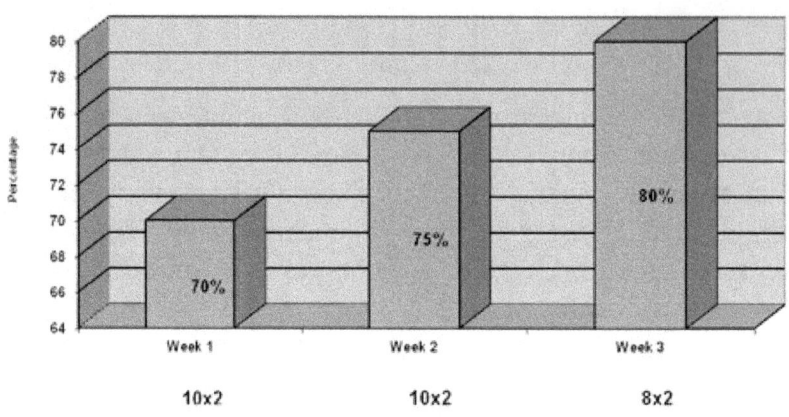

Figure 2.3. This graph shows percentages for weeks one through three.

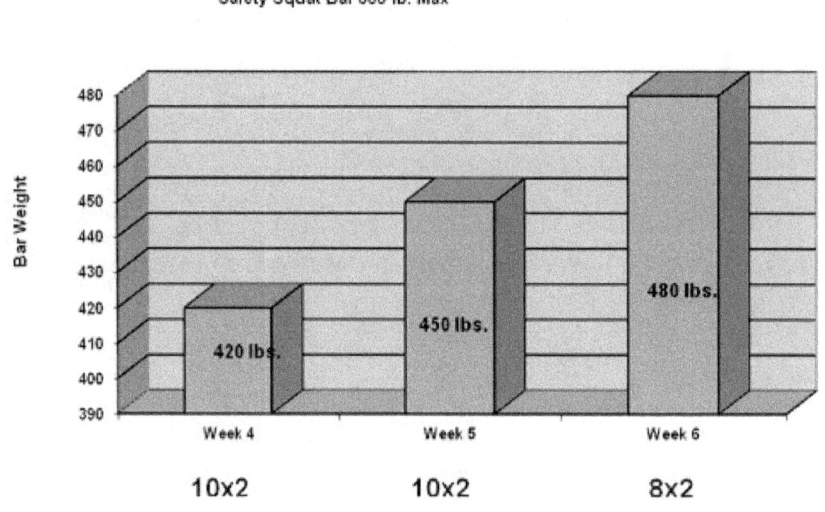

Figure 2.4. This graph shows bar weight for weeks four through six.

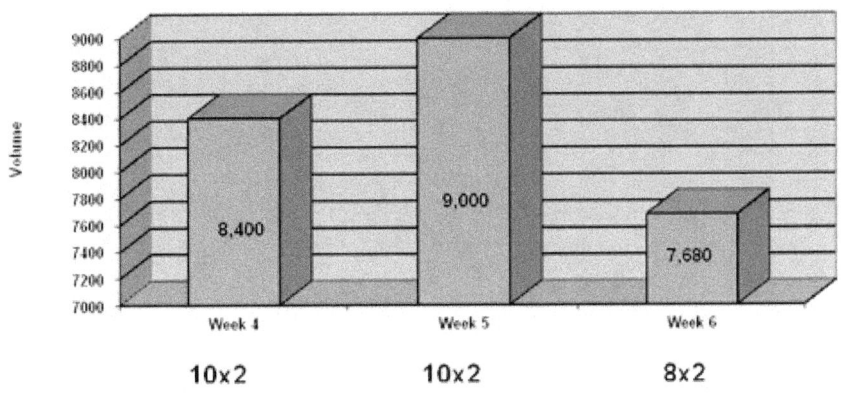

Figure 2.5. This graph shows volume for weeks four through six.

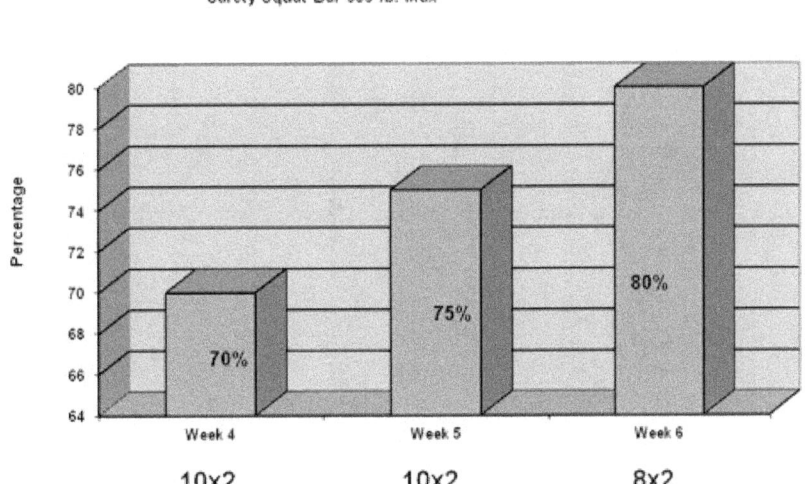

Figure 2.6. This graph shows percentages for weeks four through six.

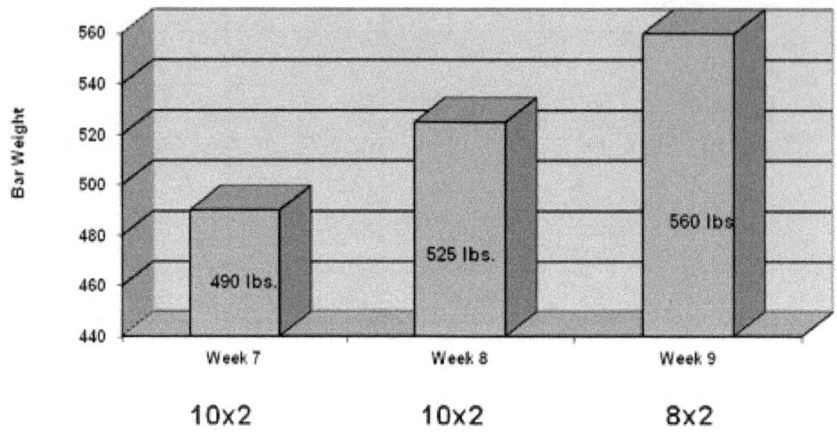

Figure 2.7. This graph shows bar weight for weeks seven through nine.

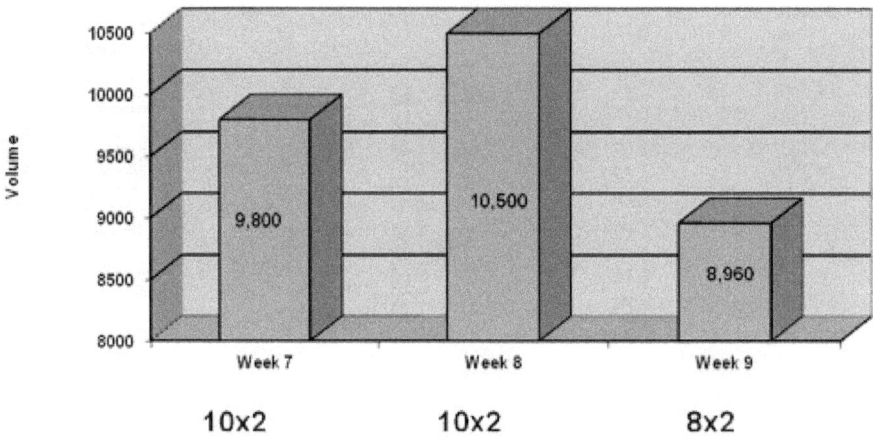

Figure 2.8. This graph shows volume for weeks seven through nine.

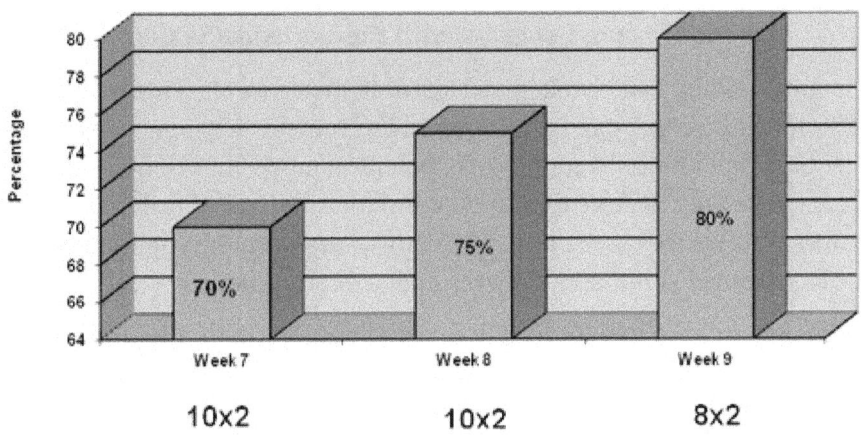

Figure 2.9. This graph shows percentages for weeks seven through nine.

More Wave Cycle Discussion

The wave cycles vary as bands, chains, or combinations of both are added to the barbell to accommodate resistance. When using weight releasers, the added weight on the first eccentric rep phase can be calculated. The variations of a wave are too numerous to list.

The speed strength waves for squatting, jerk, and press normally last three weeks, and the strength speed waves last only two weeks due to their severity as well as the near max or circa-max wave phases. If the speed day waves are of ultra-high volume for squatting with speed pulls following, the squats are also of high volume workout. A speed strength squat day is followed by a maximal effort day 72 hours later; then, a high volume squat and deadlift follows 72 hours afterwards, then they deload. Most can only sustain three max effort workouts in a row. On deload day, work on special exercises or form.

The next schedule max effort is replaced by a Repetition Method workout to recover from the severity of such training. Then, embark on as heavy a workload for three or four more workouts. For the squat and pull, this approach works for the pressing days as well, such as standing press or some form of bench pressing flat or angled. Remember when you feel mentally or physically exhausted, replace the normal speed or max effort workouts with a repetition workout designed for working the less fatigued muscle groups. Repetition work means lots of extensions for the back, hips, arms and trunk.

Note to reader: Speed strength cycles last two or three weeks progressively, going higher in percentage and somewhat higher volume. On max effort days, the barbell exercise must change each week. Example: One week is a squat exercise, a pulling exercise the next, followed by a Goodmorning exercise and occasionally, a repetition day thrown in for recovery for overtaxed muscles. These are in no particular order. Exercises must be chosen for individual goals. Again, repetition work must consist of single joint exercises. Examples exercises are back raises, glute/ham raises, tripes extensions, and the like.

Unlike many athletes who have a yearly or even a multi-year plan or the plan and methodology for an Olympic cycle, it is planned with a timetable for developing certain systems. Their concept is to increase intensity while lowering volume, making a functional plan on how fast an individual will be, how high he can jump, or how much he can lift at a particular date during the year. Then and only then will progress be noted. Is the athlete ahead or behind schedule?

Monitoring Progress with the Westside System

The Westside system of training can check speed strength every week. This is done with the three-week pendulum wave. Explosive strength can be monitored the same as jumping progress. Maximal strength for upper and lower body is monitored each week. Potential new PRs can be done at over 90 percent sometimes 95 percent year-long. Remember to note the four periods of training—accumulation, intensification, transformation and delayed transformation—are used only in the beginning of training. Then, all aspects are combined simultaneously through a yearly plan.

The Westside system prepares the athlete for the delayed transformation period or the circa-max phase that Westside uses for power meets. It is a wave of the highest intensity; hopefully, a new record of some type is set, depending on the sport. The critical delayed transformation phase or the de-loading phase trains from explosive to maximal strength, covering all elements of strength: coordination, fitness, flexibility, raising lactic acid, aerobic and anaerobic, threshold barriers while increasing V02 max. All components can and must be trained simultaneously. Delayed transformation was adapted from track and field, and from Olympic weightlifters from the former Soviet Union.

Periodization can be a weekly, monthly or yearly plan. This plan can lead to a four-year or an Olympic cycle. Speaking of Olympic cycles, a college athlete sports career can be four years for improving leg and back strength, and there must be a mathematical system to follow. Westside has used the wave system of periodization for more than 30 years with great success. It is, of course, a math problem to be addressed that combines bar speed, total volume and precise intensity zones of a predetermined percent of a one rep max. This along with proper biomechanics and physics can spell certain success. One such plan is outlined next.

The Plan: From a 400- to a 1,000-Pound Squat

400-Pound Max Squat

Percent	Weight (pounds)	Reps	Lifts	Band Tension	Volume
50%	200	12x2	24	25%	4,800 lb
55%	220	12x2	24	25%	5,280 lb
60%	240	10x2	20	25%	4,800 lb
Bar Speed is 0.8 m/s avg.					

450-Pound Max Squat

Percent	Weight (pounds)	Reps	Lifts	Band Tension	Volume
50%	225	12x2	24	25%	5,400 lb
55%	250	12x2	24	25%	6,000 lb
60%	270	10x2	20	25%	5,400 lb
Bar Speed is 0.8 m/s avg.					

500-Pound Max Squat

Percent	Weight (pounds)	Reps	Lifts	Band Tension	Volume
50%	250	12x2	24	25%	6,000 lb
55%	275	12x2	24	25%	6,600 lb
60%	300	10x2	20	25%	6,000 lb
Bar Speef is 0.8 m/s avg.					

550-Pound Max Squat

Percent	Weight (pounds)	Reps	Lifts	Band Tension	Volume
50%	275	12x2	24	25%	6,600 lb
55%	300	12x2	24	25%	7,200 lb
60%	330	10x2	20	25%	6,600 lb
Bar Speed is 0.8 m/s avg.					

600-Pound Max Squat

Percent	Weight (pounds)	Reps	Lifts	Band Tension	Volume
50%	300	12x2	24	25%	7,200 lb
55%	330	12x2	24	25%	7,920 lb
60%	360	10x2	20	25%	7,200 lb
Bar Speed is 0.8 m/s avg.					

650-Pound Max Squat

Percent	Weight (pounds)	Reps	Lifts	Band Tension	Volume
50%	325	12x2	24	25%	7,800 lb
55%	355	12x2	24	25%	8,520 lb
60%	390	10x2	20	25%	7,800 lb
Bar Speed is 0.8 m/s avg.					

700-Pound Max Squat

Percent	Weight (pounds)	Reps	Lifts	Band Tension	Volume
50%	350	12x2	24	25%	8,400 lb
55%	385	12x2	24	25%	9,240 lb
60%	420	10x2	20	25%	8,400 lb
Bar Speed is 0.8 m/s avg.					

750-Pound Max Squat

Percent	Weight (pounds)	Reps	Lifts	Band Tension	Volume
50%	375	12x2	24	25%	9,000 lb
55%	425	12x2	24	25%	10,200 lb
60%	450	10x2	20	25%	9,000 lb
Bar Speed is 0.8 m/s avg.					

800-Pound Max Squat

Percent	Weight (pounds)	Reps	Lifts	Band Tension	Volume
50%	400	12x2	24	25%	9,600 lb
55%	440	12x2	24	25%	10,560 lb
60%	480	10x2	20	25%	9,600 lb
Bar Speed is 0.8 m/s avg.					

850-Pound Max Squat

Percent	Weight (pounds)	Reps	Lifts	Band Tension	Volume
50%	425	12x2	24	25%	10,200 lb
55%	470	12x2	24	25%	11,280 lb
60%	510	10x2	20	25%	10,200 lb
Bar Speed is 0.8 m/s avg.					

900-Pound Max Squat

Percent	Weight (pounds)	Reps	Lifts	Band Tension	Volume
50%	450	12x2	24	25%	10,800 lb
55%	495	12x2	24	25%	11,880 lb
60%	540	10x2	20	25%	10,800 lb
Bar Speed is 0.8 m/s avg.					

950-Pound Max Squat

Percent	Weight (pounds)	Reps	Lifts	Band Tension	Volume
50%	475	12x2	24	25%	11,400 lb
55%	520	12x2	24	25%	12,480 lb
60%	570	10x2	20	25%	11,400 lb
Bar Speed is 0.8 m/s avg.					

1000-Pound Max Squat

Percent	Weight (pounds)	Reps	Lifts	Band Tension	Volume
50%	500	12x2	24	25%	12,000 lb
55%	550	12x2	24	25%	13,200 lb
60%	600	10x2	20	25%	12,000 lb
Bar Speed is 0.8 m/s avg.					

Notice the bar speed is constant, roughly .8 m/s. Secondly, it requires a total of 600 pounds of volume to increase the squat 50 pounds, and the percent range is 50 percent to 60 percent. The rep range and total number of lifts remain the same. The amount of band tension or chains is also constant. The three-week waves for a period of time yields the 50-pound increase by building maximal strength on max effort day, 72 hours later plus special exercises.

By studying these graphs carefully, it can be seen how mathematics plays a large role in gaining strength and force production.

Let's look at the total volume for a 400-pound max squat. It is one-half of the total volume of an 800-pound max squat. A 400-pound max squat requires one to maintain 4,800 pounds of volume; whereas, 800 pounds involves 9,600 pounds of volume. This is twice as much as a 400-pound squat. A 500-pound squatter must maintain 6,000 pounds of volume. It takes 12,000 pounds to maintain a 1,000-pound squat, which is exactly twice the volume. While the goal as a coach may be to maintain a squat max of 400 pounds or 700 pounds for a lineman to be able to ensure the force development of the before-mentioned squat, the appropriate volume must be adhered to. This is a proven method of strength training, which is referred to as the Dynamic Method.

The primary goal is to develop a fast rate of force development in sports of all kinds. For those who use a Tendo unit, speed strength is the goal of 0.8 to 0.9 m/s average. Speed strength is trained at intermediate velocities. Know at what velocity a particular special strength is trained at or failure will ensue while attempting to improve a special strength. These speeds can be found on page 150 in Mel Siff's *Supertraining*, 2003.

To avoid accommodation in volume in a weekly plan, the special exercises will fluctuate to such an extent that accommodation is impossible. A second method is to change the total volume while training at a certain percent while using a three-week wave and a cycle is to use a special bar at the same percent. The workload can change. It is evident that a particular percent—this time 50 percent—can greatly change the work load when doing a back squat compared to a front squat or an overhead squat. The example shows that a typical 500 back squatter would normally have a max front squat of 350 pounds and an overhead squat of an estimated 250 pounds. When looking at the first week wave at 50 percent in the three different squat styles, the total volume per set of two reps would be respectively 500 pounds, 350 pounds, and 250 pounds.

Changing Volume While Maintaining Bar Speed

Max	Percent	Weight (pounds)	Volume
500 lb back squat	50%	250	500 lb per set
350 lb front squat	50%	175	350 lb per set
250 lb overhead squat	50%	125	250 lb per set

This is the simplest way to change volume while maintaining bar speed at the predetermined bar speed at the fixed weekly percent. For more examples, the three graphs below show using chains for a 400-pound max squat; a 600-pound max squat; and an 800-pound max squat. For benching, the bar weight remains the same, but the accommodating resistance changes accordingly as maximum strength goes up.

Band Jerk and Press Workout for Speed Strength

300 Max Percentage

Percent	Weight (pounds)	Reps	Band Tension	Total Volume
50%	150	9x3 Reps	75 lb	4,050 lb
50%	150	9x3 Reps	75 lb	4,050 lb
50%	150	9x3 Reps	75 lb	4,050 lb

400 Max Percentage

Percent	Weight (pounds)	Reps	Band Tension	Total Volume
50%	200	9x3 Reps	100 lb	5,400 lb
50%	200	9x3 Reps	100 lb	5,400 lb
50%	200	9x3 Reps	100 lb	5,400 lb

450 Max Percentage

Percent	Weight (pounds)	Reps	Band Tension	Total Volume
50%	225	9x3 Reps	125 lb	6,000 lb
50%	225	9x3 Reps	125 lb	6,000 lb
50%	225	9x3 Reps	125 lb	6,000 lb

These charts are guidelines for not only squatting, pulling, and pressing, but variations of the Olympic lifts or the deadlift. It should teach proper planning order to control volume and intensity zones and suitable bar speed.

Periodization by Percentages

Westside constantly talks about the value of controlling loading by a percentage of a one rep max. This solves the problem of overtraining or detraining. I found the importance of this after applying the advice of A.S. Prilepin's chart for loading at different percentages in *Managing the Training of Weightlifters*. He listed how many repetitions per set as well as how many lifts per workout. His findings show that if the number of lifts are vastly under or over, the training effect decreases. The subject can be thoroughly studied in this book. A sound conclusion was discussed there by A.S. Medvedev's in a section titled "*A System of Multi-Year Training in Weightlifting.*"

At the 1964 Olympics, Leonid Zhabotinsky had won the gold medal. Zhabotinsky's volume remained the same for the next two years although his intensity decreased. The result of this was no increase in his total. In 1967, the training intensity was raised and once again the totals started to rise. How does a sportsman increase his lift without overtraining or detraining while maintaining correct bar speed? The answer, a three-week pendulum wave for speed strength development because it controls volume and intensity for one's strength level.

Below is an outline of a 50 pound jump to raise a squat from 400 pounds to 700 pounds. If strength and speed have not increased by a great deal, the athlete and coach have failed.

400-Pound Max Squat

Percent	Weight (pounds)	Reps	Lifts	Band Tension	Volume
50%	200	12x2	24	25%	4,800 lb
55%	220	12x2	24	25%	5,280 lb
60%	240	10x2	20	25%	4,800 lb
Bar Speed is 0.8 m/s avg.					

450-Pound Max Squat

Percent	Weight (pounds)	Reps	Lifts	Band Tension	Volume
50%	225	12x2	24	25%	5,400 lb
55%	250	12x2	24	25%	6,000 lb
60%	270	10x2	20	25%	5,400 lb
Bar Speed is 0.8 m/s avg.					

500-Pound Max Squat

Percent	Weight (pounds)	Reps	Lifts	Band Tension	Volume
50%	250	12x2	24	25%	6,000 lb
55%	275	12x2	24	25%	6,600 lb
60%	300	10x2	20	25%	6,000 lb
Bar Speef is 0.8 m/s avg.					

550-Pound Max Squat

Percent	Weight (pounds)	Reps	Lifts	Band Tension	Volume
50%	275	12x2	24	25%	6,600 lb
55%	300	12x2	24	25%	7,200 lb
60%	330	10x2	20	25%	6,600 lb
Bar Speed is 0.8 m/s avg.					

600-Pound Max Squat

Percent	Weight (pounds)	Reps	Lifts	Band Tension	Volume
50%	300	12x2	24	25%	7,200 lb
55%	330	12x2	24	25%	7,920 lb
60%	360	10x2	20	25%	7,200 lb
Bar Speed is 0.8 m/s avg.					

650-Pound Max Squat

Percent	Weight (pounds)	Reps	Lifts	Band Tension	Volume
50%	325	12x2	24	25%	7,800 lb
55%	355	12x2	24	25%	8,520 lb
60%	390	10x2	20	25%	7,800 lb
Bar Speed is 0.8 m/s avg.					

700-Pound Max Squat

Percent	Weight (pounds)	Reps	Lifts	Band Tension	Volume
50%	350	12x2	24	25%	8,400 lb
55%	385	12x2	24	25%	9,240 lb
60%	420	10x2	20	25%	8,400 lb
Bar Speed is 0.8 m/s avg.					

Look at the waves carefully. The bar speed remains the same during each wave regardless of the bar weight. Why is it important regardless if it is 400-pound max as a freshman or a 700-pound max as a senior? Accommodating resistance with bands or chains must be implemented to promote accelerating strength. If strength does not increase, speed won't increase either. To become stronger, volume must increase at the same intensity zones. Each max has a correct amount of volume. Just like the great Olympic champion, L. Zhabotinsky, found if volume stays the same, the results will stagnate. This multi-year system perfects skills as strength is increased, and one should be able to use perfect form while using moderate weights. Remember the equation $F=ma$. Three days or 72 hours later, a max effort day must occur. This builds absolute strength.

While experts like A.P. Bondarchuk theory is by perfecting skills, an individual utilizes strength gains. My idea is to increase muscular strength to perfect skills by increasing coordination. I am sure neither Bondarchuk nor I are totally correct, but this system blends both together. This system is simple mathematics.

Look at the raise in strength at 50-pound intervals and the volume climbs 600 pounds at the same intensities. Let's look at the bench press although any style of pressing can use this system, such as: overhead press, push jerk in front or behind head. The bench waves stay at one constant percent with barbell weight. The change in resistance is made by changing the amount of bands, chains or weight releasers.

Four Examples of a Three-Week Wave

300-pound Max Clean/Snatch

Percent	Weight (pounds)	Reps	Lifts	Total Volume
50%	150	9x3	27	85 lb
50%	150	9x3	27	85 lb
50%	150	9x3	27	85 lb

300-pound Max Clean/Snatch

Percent	Weight (pounds)	Reps	Lifts	Total Volume
50%	150	9x3	27	80 lb
50%	150	9x3	27	80 lb
50%	150	9x3	27	80 lb

300-pound Max Clean/Snatch

Percent	Weight (pounds)	Reps	Lifts	Chain Weight and Band Tension
50%	150	9x3	27	80 lb; 25 lb at top
50%	150	9x3	27	80 lb; 25 lb at top
50%	150	9x3	27	80 lb; 25 lb at top

300-pound Max Clean/Snatch
Lightened Method

Percent	Weight (pounds)	Reps	Lifts	Unload Weight
80%	240	9x3	27	60 lb
80%	240	9x3	27	60 lb
80%	240	9x3	27	60 lb

As can be seen in the four examples, it is the method of accommodating resistance so to develop maximal tension throughout the entire range of motion. Many times exercise machines use a special cam with variable lever arms as to apply a larger force at the weakest point of the strength curve (V.M. Zatsiorsky). This is done with varying totals of band tension, chain weight or using the lightened method with different amounts of unloading in the bottom. Real weight must be employed. Machines build muscle, not motion. Always use three different grips, none being outside the power lines.

SPEED PULLS

Westside uses three types of speed pulls after speed squats:

1. Speed pulls on floor with bands

The math is roughly 30 percent band tension at lockout plus 50 percent bar weight of a one rep max. A 700-pound deadlifter would use a 345 pound bar weight plus 220 pounds at top of lift. A three-week wave would look like this:

700-Pound Deadlift

Wide Sumo on Floor				
Week	Weight (pounds)	Reps	Sets	Band Tension
1	345	3	10	220 lb
2	345	8	8	220 lb
3	345	6	6	220 lb

700-Pound Deadlift

Conventional Rack Pulls with Bands				
Week	Weight (pounds)	Reps	Sets	Band Tension
4	345	2	10	250 lb
5	345	2	8	250 lb
6	345	2	6	250 lb

700-Pound Deadlift

Close Sumo on Floor				
Week	Weight (pounds)	Reps	Sets	Band Tension
7	345	1	10	280 lb
8	345	1	8	280 lb
9	345	1	6	280 lb

700-Pound Deadlift

Conventional Rack Pulls				
Week	Weight (pounds)	Reps	Sets	Band Tension
10	315	3	10	350 lb
11	315	3	8	350 lb
12	315	3	6	350 lb

2. **Ultra wide sumo deadlifts with bar weight**

700-Pound Deadlift

Ultra Wide Sumo with Barbell weight			
Week	Weight (pounds)	Reps	Sets
13	500	3	10
14	500	3	8
15	500	3	6

Notice how a three-week wave is constantly altered to avoid accommodation. The weight may vary or the stance may change from sumo to conventional to ultra wide sumo to rack pulls.

3. **Box deadlifts**

Considering box deadlifts, I suggest placing bar on mats to raise the elevation of the barbell. This maintains the feel of the mechanics of the bar. The band tension also changes each cycle or on the fourth week. The loading graphs are based on a 700-pound max deadlift. All one needs is to do reduce the amount of bar weight and band tension by 50 percent.

350-Pound Deadlift

Wide Sumo on Floor 350-Pound Deadlift				
Week	Weight (pounds)	Reps	Sets	Band Tension
1	175	1	10	110 lb
2	175	1	8	110 lb
3	175	1	6	110 lb

350-Pound Deadlift

Conventional Rack Pulls with Bands				
Week	Weight (pounds)	Reps	Sets	Band Tension
4	175	2	10	125 lb
5	175	2	8	125 lb
6	175	2	6	125 lb

350-Pound Deadlift

Close Sumo on Floor				
Week	Weight (pounds)	Reps	Sets	Band Tension
7	175	1	10	140 lb
8	175	1	8	140 lb
9	175	1	6	140 lb

350-Pound Deadlift

Conventional Rack Pull				
Week	Weight (pounds)	Reps	Sets	Band Tension
10	160	3	10	175 lb
11	160	3	8	175 lb
12	160	3	6	175 lb

350-Pound Deadlift

Ultra Wide Sumo with Barbell weight			
Week	Weight (pounds)	Reps	Sets
13	175	3	10
14	175	3	8
15	175	3	6

Again, note that each three-week wave is somehow different. It may be the bar weight, it can be band tension, or it could be altered by a different stance or how far the bar is off of the floor. By using a power rack or by placing plates on rubber mats, one can also stand on a 2-inch or 4-inch box. A 350-pound deadlift is half or 50 percent of the volume of a 700-pound deadlift. Mathematics is an essential part of weightlifting because a lifter must control the total volume of a training session. The intensity zones or what percent of a one rep max must also be considered. As graphs in this text show the volume must be highest on speed strength day while the intensities are moderately low to moderate—50 percent to 80 percent. The max effort day would require the intensity zone to possibly be 100 percent plus, allowing the volume to be as low as 35 percent to 50 percent. The loading for power cleans and power snatches without bands or chains must also be regulated.

The training of top weightlifters must use a wide variety of exercises, not just power cleans and power snatches, but the classical clean, jerk and snatch. More than 50 percent of all training must be comprised of special exercises such as: back raises, belt squats, inverse curls, box jumps, Reverse Hypers®, Goodmornings, and a wide variety of pulls, squats, jerks and presses.

The Soviets were experts at calculating volume and intensities. Men like A.S. Prilepin, A.D. Ermakov and N.S. Atanasov provided studies in managing and training of weightlifters that determined how many snatch and clean jerks were to be done in a single workout and how many reps, sets, and at what percent these should be monitored. Although my observations are very close to theirs, I find it is important to train optimally, not maximally or minimally. Plus, we keep percents for weightlifting five percent lower than their recommendations. The data from 1975 by A.D. Ermakov and N.S. Atansov in *Managing and Training of Weightlifters* found roughly 50 percent of the lifts fell between 75 percent and 85 percent. While it is fully recognized this is where speed strength is developed, many lifters today did not grow up doing weight lifting. I propose performing five percent less on each three-week wave.

EXAMPLE:

300-Pound Power Clean				
Week	Percent	Reps	Sets	Lifts
1	70%	3	6	18
2	75%	3	6	18
3	80%	3	4	12

This workout can be done after Friday's speed squat workout. Rest between sets about 90 seconds. This requires good GPP. After all, you are an athlete, right?

250-Pound Power Snatch

250-Pound Power Snatch				
Week	Percent	Reps	Sets	Lifts
1	70%	3	6	18
2	75%	3	6	18
3	80%	3	4	12

This workout can follow a max effort workout on Monday. First, do a max exercise. Example: Low box squats, overhead squat, Goodmornings, box pulls, rack pulls, heavy sled pulls for 60 yards, then rest 90 seconds. After a heavy lift, a clean or snatch feels lighter and faster. Add variety like band tension of different amounts. I give credit to three great men: Ermakov, Atanasov and Prilephin's in *Managing and Training of Weightlifters,* and Verkhoshansky and Medvedev in *A System of Multi-Year Training in Weightlifting,* for not only guiding my career since 1983, but undoubtedly saving my lifting lift. I have slightly modified the volume and intensity by using somewhat lighter lifts. One reason is due to a lesser background in GPP and physical preparedness, and second, we use a lot of powerlifting exercises.

A lifter must wave back down after a three-week wave, but also change something, at least slightly. Vary the amount of bar weight, band tension, chains, weight, box height, pin height, or bars to avoid accommodation. The speed day volume will be the highest while intensity will be at a low 40 percent to moderate 80 percent. Seventy-two hours later on max effort day, requires intensity to be a max of that particular day, hopefully meaning a near all-time max or an all-time max on some special exercise. It is gaining strength in the right special exercises that brings forth a next personal best in a clean or snatch or jerk.

If an individual fully understands the process or percents, he will never over train or under train. He needs to alternate weak muscle groups that lead to injuries and constantly make progress until he reaches his sport's potential. Use three, three-week waves before trying a new max. In the beginning, progress is easy, but as an individual starts to lift weights that only a handful have ever lifted, it becomes more difficult. It's lonely at the top.

For the weightlifter, it is most important to raise absolute strength to overcome larger loads; to become faster is secondary to strength. This is a common misconception of weightlifting coaches in the United States. After all, world record weights move slower than training weights. An athlete must use the optimal weight for his strength. The amount of work and rest must be monitored as well as movement tempo. Weightlifting requires a great deal of speed and strength. While speed is of course a major factor, speed is necessary to lift with strength speed for the development of quick strength.

Weights are 100 percent plus of a max lift. This can be and should be done on max effort workout days. As strength and speed increase at each percent, an individual achieves a new max to work from. This yields a larger training volume. Consider the chart that shows how a 400-max squat volume was 4,800 pounds, and how a 500-max squat would require 6,000 pounds of volume. For every 50 pounds gained in a max squat, a rise in volume of 600 pounds will be factored in at the same 50 percent to 60 percent. There is much to consider when perfecting form: GPP, recovery methods, relaxation, and above all a selection of the correct special exercises for the individual. Mental, physical, and emotional maturity needs to be considered. Many require a plan. This is a plan for an individual's current strength level and how to raise it correctly. The amount of rest between sets must be a factor because this can be critical for recovery. The percent of a one rep max and the volume the training plan calls for is imperative. This is the interval method, much like track athletes use.

With small weights that football players use for speed development, the rest between sets of two reps represents the majority of football plays four to seven seconds. An individual should and must recover in 40 seconds for 12 sets of two reps. For explosive strength development, 24 sets of two reps can be performed with 40 second intervals, which builds explosive strength in a fatigue state and represents training at 70 percent to 85 percent. The rest must be 60 seconds to 90 seconds between sets. Max effort work can require two to four minutes rest between singles, which is dependent of the athlete's level of physical preparedness.

The findings of experts like A.S. Prilepin in *Managing and Training of Weightlifters* discovered too many reps per set can change a reduction in force development. It is best to perform high sets and low reps for recovery. The high rep sets should only include special exercises for individual muscles. While his recommendation was with weights at 70 percent to 90 percent, I have concluded that 40 percent to 60 percent provides the same results. If one watches a ball bounce with every preceding bounce, the rebound has less height. Why? It's due to the loss of kinetic energy.

The human body works in a similar fashion with the expenditure of kinetic energy in the soft tissue and muscle fatigue. Repetitions range for explosive strength or explosive power. Starting strength is inherited due to the amount or ratio of fast and slow twitch muscle fiber in the body. The same holds true for absolute strength where one lifts his maximum weight with no time limit. After years of following the guidelines set forth by A.S. Prilepin, A.D. Ermakov, N.S. Atanasov and many other sports experts from the former Soviet Union and along with my own experience over 50 years, I have suggestions for planning sets, reps per workout at a predetermined intensity zone for any athlete after a period of three years of general preparation.

If bar speed is reduced, the set must be stopped because of a power reduction. Pay close attention to the minimal and maximal total reps and amount of lifts per workout. For most, the optimal number of lifts is more beneficial.

Percent	Reps	Lifts
40%	4-8	36
50%	3-6	36
60%	3-6	30
70%	3-6	18
80%	2-4	15
90%	1-2	4-10

If you are greatly above or below the optimal number, the training affects are diminished. These are the recommendations of Louie Simmons, the author. 40% no less than 24 and no more than 48
50% no less than 24 and no more than 48
60% no less than 20 and no more than 40
70% no less than 12 and no more than 24
80% no less than 10 and no more than 20
90% no less than 4 and no more than 10

How To Change Volume at the Same Intensity Zone

Increase your three maxes for a front squat, safety squat bar, and of course, a regular squat bar max. Here is how:

500-pound Max Front Squat

Week	Percent	Weight (pounds)	Reps	Lifts	Volume
1	50%	250	12X2	24	6,000 lb
2	55%	275	12X2	24	6,600 lb
3	60%	300	10X2	20	6,000 lb
Bar Speed is 0.8 m/s avg.					

600-pound Max Safety Squat Bar

Week	Percent	Weight (pounds)	Reps	Lifts	Volume
1	50%	300	12X2	24	7,200 lb
2	55%	330	12X2	24	7,920 lb
3	60%	360	10X2	20	7,200 lb
Bar Speed is 0.8 m/s avg.					

700-pound Max Regular Squat Bar

Week	Percent	Weight (pounds)	Reps	Lifts	Volume
1	50%	350	12X2	24	8,400 lb
2	55%	385	12X2	24	9,240 lb
3	60%	420	10X2	20	8,400 lb
Bar Speed is 0.8 m/s avg.					

You must pay close attention to these graphs for continued progress in classical barbell lifts including the following: Olympic weightlifting lifts, powerlifting lifts, special squats, Goodmornings, pulls and pressing exercises. Combining mathematics, physics, and biomechanics, your true potential can be reached.

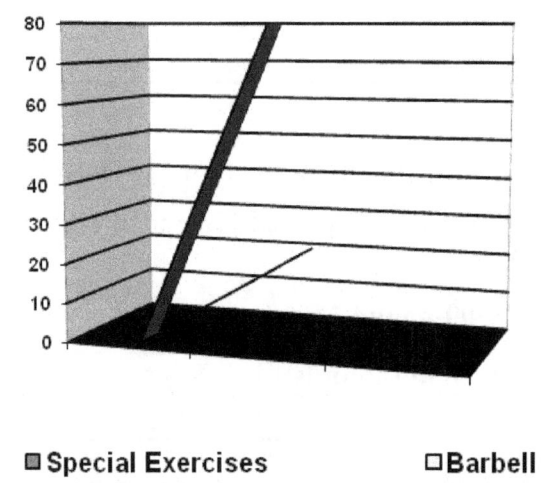

■ Special Exercises □ Barbell

Figure 3: As you can see by this chart, the ratio between barbell and classical lifts is 20 percent barbell exercises and 80 percent special exercises. This is proven by the research done at Westside Barbell by Joe Lasko on powerlifts and Olympic weightlifting as well as track and field. Because athletes are built biomechanically different it can be dangerous to perform high repetition barbell lifts, as the weakest component of the human can become fatigued and sustain injuries. It is much safer to do special exercises directed to a particular muscle group that may be lacking.

Circa Max
Performed to a parallel box.

Max Weight	Bar Weight	Weight Percent	Band Tension	Band Tension
800 lb	500 lb	62%	375 lb	47%
850 lb	550 lb	65%	375 lb	44%
900 lb	600 lb	66%	375 lb	42%
950 lb	650 lb	68%	375 lb	39%
1000 lb	600 lb	60%	440 lb	44%
1050 lb	650 lb	62%	440 lb	42%
1100 lb	700 lb	64%	440 lb	40%
1150 lb	750 lb	65%	440 lb	38%

DELAYED TRANSFORMATION CONNECTING CIRCA-MAX PHASE

The data derived in this section is from:

-Ivan Abadzhiev

-VY Verkhoshansky

-A.S. Medvedev

The results at the contest, of course, are of most importance. It requires two proven methods of periodization.

First, delayed transformation is a period of reducing the amount of volume and reducing the intensity zone somewhat to induce the highest level of sporting skill at contest time.

It was brought about through track and field and Olympic weight lifting from the former Soviet Union. For the squat training, it starts at 35 days out from contest date. Roughly 50 percent sets are done for the optimal amount of sets and lifts. The same is true for 28 days out of your contest.

Now it is interrupted at 21 days, but for Westside, it is a new or all-time record on a box squat. See the circa-max chart above and circa-max meaning near max. A circa-max phase is performed with weights in the range of 90 percent to 97 percent of a one rep max. The number of lifts at those percentages are four minimal, seven optimal and 10 maximal. Westside uses the optimal method, utilizing seven lifts on the circa max day.

An 800-pound squatter after a warm up performs the following:
- 330-pound bar weight x two reps + 375 pounds band tension
- 370-pound bar weight x two reps + 375 pounds band tension
- 420-pound bar weight x one rep + 375 pounds band tension
- 470-pound bar weight x one rep + 375 pounds band tension
- P.R. 510-pound bar weight x one rep + 375 pounds band tension

If an athlete can perform this weight, and if the box height is correct (parallel and good form), he will break a new squat record. During the second week of circa-max, the lifter will work up to approximately 370 pounds for a single.

This concludes the circa-max phase. It represents 21 days out and 14 days out. Now more recovery time is needed. Seven days out large men (275 pounds and up) will not squat, but do only special exercises. Two hundred and forty two pound men and lighter can squat light. For example, 330 pounds x 2 x 2 with no band tension or if you like 140lb of band tension.

As you see, Westside divides the delayed transformation phase in two parts: with extreme stimulus at 21 days out, then back to the delayed transformation through 14 days out to assure all three lifts are at their max on contest day. **Refer to chart 3.1 on page 54** for an explanation of our combination method training by using bands on and bar weight.

This chart is the combined efforts of 75 men who have officially squatted from 800 pounds up to 1,205 pounds. Look carefully at the bar weight percentage and the band tension percentage.

As a lifter progresses from 800 pounds to 950 pounds, the bar percentage goes from 62 percent to 68 percent, causing the band tension to go from 47 percent to 39 percent. This means the bar percent goes up six percent while the band tension goes down eight percent. Let it be noted as well that at 1,000 pounds to 1,150 pounds, the bar percent goes up five percent while the band tension goes down six percent.

I am asked about scientific studies and I can tell you that no one besides Westside has such a study with world class strength athletes. Ours is a work of more than twenty years of experiments. More can be learned about the Delayed Transformation Phase on pg. 30 in *Science and Practice of Strength Training* (Zatsiorsky Circa Max Method 1995; Yerkhoshansky 2009 Supertraining).

Workouts

1. Clean pull, followed by squat clean
2. Jerk barbell taken from stands
3. Clean and jerk starting with barbell below knees
4. Push jerk followed by jerk, barbell taken from stands
5. Clean pull with four stops upwards
6. Power clean, squat, then jerk
7. Clean and jerk starting with barbell at knee level
8. Clean pull from the floor
9. Jerk from behind the head
10. Clean and jerk starting with barbell below the knees
11. Push jerk with barbell taken from stands
12. Clean pull with a medium hand spacing
13. Squat followed by jerk behind the head
14. Classic clean and jerk from the floor
15. Power clean starting with barbell at knee level
16. Clean pull standing on a block
17. Push jerk from behind the head followed by overhead squat
18. Front squat followed by jerk

19. Clean pull starting with the barbell at knee level
20. Power clean from the floor
21. Half jerk followed by the jerk with barbell taken from stands
22. Clean pull slowly up plus lower slowly
23. Push jerk after power clean
24. Power clean, push jerk, then overhead squat
25. Clean pull to knee level

Special Notes

PROGRESS IS BASED ON PERIODIZATION

A weightlifter has to build a strong back and legs to reach the top. I had read David Rigert could squat 10 reps with 675 pounds at 198-pound body weight. I had also read a story after bombing out of a major meet with a 352-pound snatch. David took some time off. But when he returned to a lifting hall, a lifter was snatching the same 352 pounds that he bombed out with. David's friend noticed he was glaring at the bar and realized what David was thinking and said "don't do it!" David (in street clothes) approached the bar loaded with 352 pounds and proceeded to snatch it with no warm-up. These two stories tell the author just how strong his legs and back were. This could account for David breaking world records.

I have had several novice weightlifters visit Westside to train. By the author's system of combinations of method training, they will break their record in the clean or snatch nine out of 10 times in just 30 minutes. Many times they have been stuck for months without a PR. After setting a new clean or snatch record, which is low by any standards due to low back strength, they are unable to recover from the clean (due to even lower leg strength). You must raise max strength to reach the top. Many think that speed is most important due to the fact that you can only make the lift with the amount of weight you do in the weakest portion of the lift. It does no good to clean 400 pounds if your front squat is 360 pounds or to snatch 300 pounds if your overhead squat is 280 pounds. The legs must have an over-abundance of strength compared to your clean or snatch. I constantly hear that the squat only has to be a small percent of your clean and jerk. This is completely WRONG! Not only do you have to recover from the clean, but you also have a reserve of leg strength for the thrust in the jerk.

Weightlifters in the former Soviet Union had a wide base before weight training began. This lead to at least basic leg strength. A good coach or lifter should know that the top five inter-dependent correlations for maximal results are:

1. Power Clean
2. Power Snatch
3. Clean
4. Overhead Squat
5. Clean from the Hang

This is according to *Managing the Training of Weightlifters*.

The author's findings have concluded that when the squat was raised, the pulls and any pulls increased as well. So what is the answer? It has been said that some lifters squat six times a week, but with no great results. The author has viewed several squat workouts and found they are too slow to produce proper force. The percentages should range between 75 percent and 85 percent with only barbell weight or 50 percent to 60 percent with 25 percent band tension at the top for three-week pendulum waves. The bar should move at .8 to .9 m/s—this is force equals mass times acceleration. I hope this sounds familiar as it is Newton's Second Law of F=MA Why is this so important? Let's look at the definition of work:

In physics, work is defined as the product of net force and the displacement throughout where that force is exerted or W=F. If work is a barbell lift, clean, or squat, then how can one move the same or larger weight faster? The answer: by becoming more powerful. In physics, power is divided by the time used to do the work or P=wt. This simply means the more powerful lifter can do the work in less time. Now we are finally getting to the point. Yes, we need a stronger squat! But squatting repeatedly is not the answer. The problem is the Law of Accommodation: meaning if one does the same exercise with the same training load repeatedly, the performance will decrease over time. Many would think this is the definition of insanity, but science refers to it as accommodation, a biological law.

The pulls are the same. They, too, will stop increasing poundages if done repeatedly. The Westside conjugate system calls for breaking down the squats and pulls into segments. You must increase leg strength—meaning calves, hamstrings, and quads—into special exercises for each muscle group.

SPECIAL EXERCISES:
- Leg Presses
- Step Ups
- Glute/Ham Raises
- Inverse Curls
- Calf Raises
- Sled Pulls
- Wheel Barrows
- Back Raises
- Goodmornings
- Reverse Hypers
- Belt Squats
- Box Jumping
- Upright Rows
- Bent Over Rows
- Pull-ups

These are some small special exercises that can make an incredible difference in building a strong squat and pull.

Why does Westside want you to use a wide stance for squatting? Because you have never worked those muscles! Those unused muscles are contributing to lifting more weight. Wide stance straight leg style deadlifts and wide stance arched back power cleans, for example.

Side Note: I was having a discussion about the deadlift for Olympic lifters when a well-known author said that a powerlifting deadlift would not work for an Olympic lifter due to the round backed style. I replied "what about the sumo style where the back is arched?" He had no clue. This is the problem with most (not all) Olympic coaches—they do not have a clue about anything that can improve strength. Perfect form must be taught in the early stages then a constant increase in strength must come to win bigger and bigger contests. I hope this makes sense to you. Hardly anyone has a perfect body for any sport, especially weightlifting. Everyone has some muscle groups stronger than others. Some have very strong backs and not so strong legs. Of course, the back will do the majority of the work load. But what if that individual builds his or her legs up to match their back strength? They could, of course, lift heavier weights and be much safer, too, because the work would be distributed throughout the body.

I have asked Tom Eiseman (780 at 181 pounds) where he felt the deadlift the most and his reply was very profound. His answer was "everywhere." Only small special exercises can bring up lacking or weak muscle groups. An example is ab work. If one did no direct ab work, abs would be weak leading to back ailments. If you are very strong, but slow, you must work on your explosive and speed strength. But don't neglect your strength speed—the one thing you are blessed with. Train what you don't have. But, remember, it does no good to be strong in the wrong exercises.

If Medvedev had more than 75 barbell exercises for the weightlifter, there were of course many more small special exercises. For a single muscle group, many were on special machines; then there are Kettlebells, alternating close grips for snatches and wide grips for cleans, to name a few.

Last, but not least, please read. I have a large list of books for anyone who will read them. I used this material to build the strongest powerlifting gym in the history of powerlifting. As of July 2014, Westside had five of the top 10 totals of all time. This includes the highest total of 3,005 at 271 and the top two coefficient totals of all time. Plus, the number one women's coefficient totals of all time. Also, the top coefficient squats for men and women and the top coefficient bench press for men and women in a power meet. This Westside Method is 33 years in the making. Its methods are from weightlifting and track and field.

The author re-engineered the Soviet System to fit not only powerlifting, but all sports.

Warning: there is no such thing as five rep systems, three rep systems, or the single rep system, nor the Cube Method, 5-3-1 Method or the Nebraska System. These systems are fantasy.

There are four systems that are proven by science:

The Maximal Effort Method

The Dynamic Effort Method

The Submaximal Effort Method

The Repeated Effort Method

Westside thanks the great former Soviet Union sports scientists like V.M Zatsiorsky, and Dr. Mel Siff of *Supertraining* fame (a good friend may he rest in peace) Along with Y.V Verkhoshansky, Mel was a true genius in the development of sports science. And don't forget Dr. Isaac Newton the father of the laws of motion. Without these great men and a long list of others that are mentioned in the references, we wouldn't be where we are today.

Chapter 7: Speed Strength and Max Effort Workouts

Chapter 7: Speed Strength and Max Effort Workouts

Here is a list of speed strength and max effort workouts that are intended to be rotated in three-week waves in a multi-year program. While we did not lift, all programs were devised by Medvedev. As you can see, a total of 18 lifts per workout are used, plus you must use a speed strength wave with the squat. The waves cover the snatch, power snatch, snatch pulls, clean and jerk, power clean, and clean pulls. Remember the 20 percent classical or barbell lifts while 80% special exercises mentioned before ranging from Goodmornings, pressing, jumping, depth jumps, back raises, reverse hypers, belt squats, leg presses, and many more.

Use the pulling and squatting workouts for max effort, plus pressing and jerking exercises. Other exercises can be found in *Supertraining* 2003 sixth edition by Mel Siff

Forty Three-Week Wave Examples

- Remember a new three-week dynamic wave begins on the fourth week!

Week	Exercise	Sets	Reps	Lifts	% of 1 REP MAX
1	SNATCH	3	3	9	75%
	CLEAN	3	3	9	75%
2	SNATCH	3	3	9	80%
	CLEAN	3	3	9	80%
3	SNATCH	3	3	9	85%
	CLEAN	3	3	9	85%

Week	Exercise	Sets	Reps	Lifts	% of 1 REP MAX
1	POWER CLEAN FROM KNEES	3	3	9	75%
	SNATCH FROM HIGH BOX	3	3	9	75%
2	POWER CLEAN FROM KNEES	3	3	9	80%
	SNATCH FROM HIGH BOX	3	3	9	80%
3	POWER CLEAN FROM KNEES	3	3	9	85%
	SNATCH FROM HIGH BOX	3	3	9	85%

- Remember a new three-week dynamic wave begins on the fourth week!

Week	Exercise	Sets	Reps	Lifts	% of 1 REP MAX
1	CLASSIC SNATCH	3	3	9	75%
	HANG CLEAN	3	3	9	75%
2	CLEAN PULL FROM FLOOR	3	3	9	80%
	SNATCH BELOW THE KNEES	3	3	9	80%
3	POWER SNATCH W/OVERHEAD SQUAT	3	3	9	85%
	HANG CLEAN ABOVE THE KNEE	3	3	9	85%

Week	Exercise	Sets	Reps	Lifts	% of 1 REP MAX
1	POWER CLEAN FROM FLOOR	3	3	9	75%
	SPLIT SNATCH	3	3	9	75%
2	POWER CLEAN FROM FLOOR	3	3	9	80%
	SPLIT SNATCH	3	3	9	80%
3	POWER CLEAN FROM FLOOR	3	3	9	85%
	SPLIT SNATCH	3	3	9	85%

Week	Exercise	Sets	Reps	Lifts	% of 1 REP MAX
1	SNATCH ON A LOW BOX	3	3	9	75%
	CLEAN FROM LOW BOX	3	3	9	75%
2	SNATCH ON A LOW BOX	3	3	9	80%
	CLEAN FROM LOW BOX	3	3	9	80%
3	SNATCH ON A LOW BOX	3	3	9	85%
	CLEAN FROM LOW BOX	3	3	9	85%

Week	Exercise	Sets	Reps	Lifts	% of 1 REP MAX
1	CLEAN AND JERK W/ BARBELL AT KNEE	3	3	9	75%
	SNATCH PULL W/RISE ONTO TOES	3	3	9	75%
2	LEAN AND JERK W/ BARBELL AT KNEE	3	3	9	80%
	SNATCH PULL W/RISE ONTO TOES	3	3	9	80%
3	LEAN AND JERK W/ BARBELL AT KNEE	3	3	9	85%
	SNATCH PULL W/RISE ONTO TOES	3	3	9	85%

- Remember a new three-week dynamic wave begins on the fourth week!

Week	Exercise	Sets	Reps	Lifts	% of 1 REP MAX
1	HANG CLEAN AND JERK	3	3	9	75%
	SPLIT SNATCH	3	3	9	75%
2	HANG CLEAN AND JERK	3	3	9	80%
	SPLIT SNATCH	3	3	9	80%
3	HANG CLEAN AND JERK	3	3	9	85%
	SPLIT SNATCH	3	3	9	85%

Week	Exercise	Sets	Reps	Lifts	% of 1 REP MAX
1	RDL	3	3	9	75%
	CLEAN PULL TO KNEE LEVEL	3	3	9	75%
2	RDL	3	3	9	80%
	CLEAN PULL TO KNEE LEVEL	3	3	9	80%
3	RDL	3	3	9	85%
	CLEAN PULL TO KNEE LEVEL	3	3	9	85%

Week	Exercise	Sets	Reps	Lifts	% of 1 REP MAX
1	CLEAN PULL W/CLOSE GRIP	3	3	9	75%
	SPLIT SNATCH W/BAR BELOW KNEES	3	3	9	75%
2	CLEAN PULL W/CLOSE GRIP	3	3	9	80%
	SPLIT SNATCH W/BAR BELOW KNEES	3	3	9	80%
3	CLEAN PULL W/CLOSE GRIP	3	3	9	85%
	SPLIT SNATCH W/BAR BELOW KNEES	3	3	9	85%

Week	Exercise	Sets	Reps	Lifts	% of 1 REP MAX
1	SNATCH GRIP DEADLIFT	3	3	9	75%
	PUSH-JERK W/OVERHEAD SQUAT	3	3	9	75%
2	SNATCH GRIP DEADLIFT	3	3	9	80%
	PUSH-JERK W/OVERHEAD SQUAT	3	3	9	80%
3	SNATCH GRIP DEADLIFT	3	3	9	85%
	PUSH-JERK W/OVERHEAD SQUAT	3	3	9	85%

Week	Exercise	Sets	Reps	Lifts	% of 1 REP MAX
1	HANG CLEAN W/FRONT SQUAT	3	3	9	75%
	SNATCH PULL FOLLOWED BY CLASSIC SNATCH	3	3	9	75%
2	HANG CLEAN W/FRONT SQUAT	3	3	9	80%
	SNATCH PULL FOLLOWED BY CLASSIC SNATCH	3	3	9	80%
3	HANG CLEAN W/FRONT SQUAT	3	3	9	85%
	SNATCH PULL FOLLOWED BY CLASSIC SNATCH	3	3	9	85%

Week	Exercise	Sets	Reps	Lifts	% of 1 REP MAX
1	SNATCH PULL STARTING AT KNEES	3	3	9	75%
	CLEAN PULL FROM BELOW THE KNEES	3	3	9	75%
2	SNATCH PULL STARTING AT KNEES	3	3	9	80%
	CLEAN PULL FROM BELOW THE KNEES	3	3	9	80%
3	SNATCH PULL STARTING AT KNEES	3	3	9	85%
	CLEAN PULL FROM BELOW THE KNEES	3	3	9	85%

- Remember a new three-week dynamic wave begins on the fourth week!

Week	Exercise	Sets	Reps	Lifts	% of 1 REP MAX
1	CLASSIC SNATCH	3	3	9	75%
	CLEAN PULL FROM FLOOR	3	3	9	75%
2	CLASSIC SNATCH	3	3	9	80%
	CLEAN PULL FROM FLOOR	3	3	9	80%
3	CLASSIC SNATCH	3	3	9	85%
	CLEAN PULL FROM FLOOR	3	3	9	85%

Week	Exercise	Sets	Reps	Lifts	% of 1 REP MAX
1	POWER CLEAN TO SQUAT TO JERK	3	3	9	75%
	HANG SNATCH PULL BELOW THE KNEES	3	3	9	75%
2	POWER CLEAN TO SQUAT TO JERK	3	3	9	80%
	HANG SNATCH PULL BELOW THE KNEES	3	3	9	80%
3	POWER CLEAN TO SQUAT TO JERK	3	3	9	85%
	HANG SNATCH PULL BELOW THE KNEES	3	3	9	85%

Week	Exercise	Sets	Reps	Lifts	% of 1 REP MAX
1	SNATCH FROM ABOVE KNEES	3	3	9	75%
	JERK FROM STANDS	3	3	9	75%
2	SNATCH FROM ABOVE KNEES	3	3	9	80%
	JERK FROM STANDS	3	3	9	80%
3	SNATCH FROM ABOVE KNEES	3	3	9	85%
	JERK FROM STANDS	3	3	9	85%

Week	Exercise	Sets	Reps	Lifts	% of 1 REP MAX
1	PUSH JERK FROM BEHIND NECK FOLLOWED BY OVERHEAD SQUAT	3	3	9	75%
	SNATCH PULL FOLLOWED BY CLASSIC SNATCH	3	3	9	75%
2	PUSH JERK FROM BEHIND NECK FOLLOWED BY OVERHEAD SQUAT	3	3	9	80%
	SNATCH PULL FOLLOWED BY CLASSIC SNATCH	3	3	9	80%
3	PUSH JERK FROM BEHIND NECK FOLLOWED BY OVERHEAD SQUAT	3	3	9	85%
	SNATCH PULL FOLLOWED BY CLASSIC SNATCH	3	3	9	85%

- Remember a new three-week dynamic wave begins on the fourth week!

Week	Exercise	Sets	Reps	Lifts	% of 1 REP MAX
1	SPLIT SNATCH W/BAR AT KNEE LEVEL	3	3	9	75%
	HALF JERK FOLLOWED BY JERK TAKEN FROM STANDS	3	3	9	75%
2	SPLIT SNATCH W/BAR AT KNEE LEVEL	3	3	9	80%
	HALF JERK FOLLOWED BY JERK TAKEN FROM STANDS	3	3	9	80%
3	SPLIT SNATCH W/BAR AT KNEE LEVEL	3	3	9	85%
	HALF JERK FOLLOWED BY JERK TAKEN FROM STANDS	3	3	9	85%

Week	Exercise	Sets	Reps	Lifts	% of 1 REP MAX
1	CLEAN PULL OFF BLOCK	3	3	9	75%
	HANG SNATCH FROM ABOVE KNEES	3	3	9	75%
2	CLEAN PULL OFF BLOCK	3	3	9	80%
	HANG SNATCH FROM ABOVE KNEES	3	3	9	80%
3	CLEAN PULL OFF BLOCK	3	3	9	85%
	HANG SNATCH FROM ABOVE KNEES	3	3	9	85%

- Remember a new three-week dynamic wave begins on the fourth week!

Week	Exercise	Sets	Reps	Lifts	% of 1 REP MAX
1	CLEAN TO FRONT SQUAT	3	3	9	75%
	SNATCH PULL FROM FLOOR RISE ONTO TOES	3	3	9	75%
2	CLEAN TO FRONT SQUAT	3	3	9	80%
	SNATCH PULL FROM FLOOR RISE ONTO TOES	3	3	9	80%
3	CLEAN TO FRONT SQUAT	3	3	9	85%
	SNATCH PULL FROM FLOOR RISE ONTO TOES	3	3	9	85%

- Remember a new three-week dynamic wave begins on the fourth week!

Week	Exercise	Sets	Reps	Lifts	% of 1 REP MAX
1	HANG SNATCH BELOW KNEES	3	3	9	75%
	CLEAN PULL STANDING ON BLOCK	3	3	9	75%
2	HANG SNATCH BELOW KNEES	3	3	9	80%
	CLEAN PULL STANDING ON BLOCK	3	3	9	80%
3	HANG SNATCH BELOW KNEES	3	3	9	85%
	CLEAN PULL STANDING ON BLOCK	3	3	9	85%

Week	Exercise	Sets	Reps	Lifts	% of 1 REP MAX
1	CLEAN FROM BLOCKS BELOW KNEE	3	3	9	75%
	SNATCH PULL W/BAR AT KNEE LEVEL	3	3	9	75%
2	CLEAN FROM BLOCKS BELOW KNEE	3	3	9	80%
	SNATCH PULL W/BAR AT KNEE LEVEL	3	3	9	80%
3	CLEAN FROM BLOCKS BELOW KNEE	3	3	9	85%
	SNATCH PULL W/BAR AT KNEE LEVEL	3	3	9	85%

Week	Exercise	Sets	Reps	Lifts	% of 1 REP MAX
1	SPLIT SNATCH W/OVERHEAD SQUAT	3	3	9	75%
	CLEAN`	3	3	9	75%
2	SPLIT SNATCH W/OVERHEAD SQUAT	3	3	9	80%
	CLEAN`	3	3	9	80%
3	SPLIT SNATCH W/OVERHEAD SQUAT	3	3	9	85%
	CLEAN`	3	3	9	85%

Week	Exercise	Sets	Reps	Lifts	% of 1 REP MAX
1	CLEAN AND JERK	3	3	9	75%
	SNATCH	3	3	9	75%
2	CLEAN AND JERK	3	3	9	80%
	SNATCH	3	3	9	80%
3	CLEAN AND JERK	3	3	9	85%
	SNATCH	3	3	9	85%

Week	Exercise	Sets	Reps	Lifts	% of 1 REP MAX
1	SNATCH	3	3	9	75%
	CLEAN	3	3	9	75%
2	SNATCH	3	3	9	80%
	CLEAN	3	3	9	80%
3	SNATCH	3	3	9	85%
	CLEAN	3	3	9	85%

Note: "ACCOMMODATING RESISTANCE %" reflects tension at the top or finish position of the movement!

Week	Exercise	Sets	Reps	Lifts	% of 1 REP MAX	Accommodating Resistance %
1	POWER CLEAN TO PUSH-JERK	3	3	9	50%	25%
	SNATCH GRIP DEADLIFT TO KNEES	3	3	9	50%	25%
2	POWER CLEAN TO PUSH-JERK	3	3	9	55%	25%
	SNATCH GRIP DEADLIFT TO KNEES	3	3	9	55%	25%
3	POWER CLEAN TO PUSH-JERK	3	3	9	60%	25%
	SNATCH GRIP DEADLIFT TO KNEES	3	3	9	60%	25%

Week	Exercise	Sets	Reps	Lifts	% of 1 REP MAX	Accommodating Resistance %
1	POWER SNATCH W/ OVERHEAD SQUAT	3	3	9	50%	25%
	HANG CLEAN ABOVE KNEE	3	3	9	50%	25%
2	POWER SNATCH W/ OVERHEAD SQUAT	3	3	9	55%	25%
	HANG CLEAN ABOVE KNEE	3	3	9	55%	25%
3	POWER SNATCH W/ OVERHEAD SQUAT	3	3	9	60%	25%
	HANG CLEAN ABOVE KNEE	3	3	9	60%	25%

Week	Exercise	Sets	Reps	Lifts	% of 1 REP MAX	Accommodating Resistance %
1	CLEAN AND JERK	3	3	9	50%	25%
	SNATCH PULL FROM FLOOR	3	3	9	50%	25%
2	CLEAN AND JERK	3	3	9	55%	25%
	SNATCH PULL FROM FLOOR	3	3	9	55%	25%
3	CLEAN AND JERK	3	3	9	60%	25%
	SNATCH PULL FROM FLOOR	3	3	9	60%	25%

Week	Exercise	Sets	Reps	Lifts	% of 1 REP MAX	Accommodating Resistance %
1	SNATCH PULL PLUS SNATCH PULL FROM BELOW KNEES PLUS SNATCH PULL FROM ABOVE KNEES	3	3	9	50%	25%
	JERK FROM BEHIND HEAD	3	3	9	50%	25%
2	SNATCH PULL PLUS SNATCH PULL FROM BELOW KNEES PLUS SNATCH PULL FROM ABOVE KNEES	3	3	9	55%	25%
	JERK FROM BEHIND HEAD	3	3	9	55%	25%
3	SNATCH PULL PLUS SNATCH PULL FROM BELOW KNEES PLUS SNATCH PULL FROM ABOVE KNEES	3	3	9	60%	25%
	JERK FROM BEHIND HEAD	3	3	9	60%	25%

Week	Exercise	Sets	Reps	Lifts	% of 1 REP MAX	Accommodating Resistance %
1	WIDE GRIP POWER CLEAN	3	3	9	50%	25%
1	SNATCH PULL TO KNEES FOLLOWED BY SNATCH PULL OVER-HEAD	3	3	9	50%	25%
2	WIDE GRIP POWER CLEAN	3	3	9	55%	25%
2	SNATCH PULL TO KNEES FOLLOWED BY SNATCH PULL OVER-HEAD	3	3	9	55%	25%
3	WIDE GRIP POWER CLEAN	3	3	9	60%	25%
3	SNATCH PULL TO KNEES FOLLOWED BY SNATCH PULL OVER-HEAD	3	3	9	60%	25%

Note: "ACCOMMODATING RESISTANCE %" reflects tension at the top or finish position of the movement!

- Remember a new three-week dynamic wave begins on the fourth week!

Week	Exercise	Sets	Reps	Lifts	% of 1 REP MAX	Accommodating Resistance %
1	RDL	3	3	9	50%	25%
1	PUSH-JERK FROM STANDS OVERHEAD	3	3	9	50%	25%
2	RDL	3	3	9	55%	25%
2	PUSH-JERK FROM STANDS OVERHEAD	3	3	9	55%	25%
3	RDL	3	3	9	60%	25%
3	PUSH-JERK FROM STANDS OVERHEAD	3	3	9	60%	25%

Note: "ACCOMMODATING RESISTANCE %" reflects tension at the top or finish position of the movement!

Note: "ACCOMMODATING RESISTANCE %" reflects tension at the top or finish position of the movement!

Week	Exercise	Sets	Reps	Lifts	% of 1 REP MAX	Accommodating Resistance %
1	POWER CLEAN TO PUSH-JERK	3	3	9	50%	25%
1	SNATCH GRIP DEADLIFT TO KNEES	3	3	9	50%	25%
2	POWER CLEAN TO PUSH-JERK	3	3	9	55%	25%
2	SNATCH GRIP DEADLIFT TO KNEES	3	3	9	55%	25%
3	POWER CLEAN TO PUSH-JERK	3	3	9	60%	25%
3	SNATCH GRIP DEADLIFT TO KNEES	3	3	9	60%	25%

Week	Exercise	Sets	Reps	Lifts	% of 1 REP MAX	Accommodating Resistance %
1	POWER SNATCH W/ OVERHEAD SQUAT	3	3	9	50%	25%
1	HANG CLEAN ABOVE KNEE	3	3	9	50%	25%
2	POWER SNATCH W/ OVERHEAD SQUAT	3	3	9	55%	25%
2	HANG CLEAN ABOVE KNEE	3	3	9	55%	25%
3	POWER SNATCH W/ OVERHEAD SQUAT	3	3	9	60%	25%
3	HANG CLEAN ABOVE KNEE	3	3	9	60%	25%

Note: "ACCOMMODATING RESISTANCE %" reflects tension at the top or finish position of the movement!

- Remember a new three-week dynamic wave begins on the fourth week!

Week	Exercise	Sets	Reps	Lifts	% of 1 REP MAX	Accommodating Resistance %
1	POWER CLEAN TO PUSH-JERK	3	3	9	50%	25%
1	SNATCH GRIP DEADLIFT TO KNEES	3	3	9	50%	25%
2	POWER CLEAN TO PUSH-JERK	3	3	9	55%	25%
2	SNATCH GRIP DEADLIFT TO KNEES	3	3	9	55%	25%
3	POWER CLEAN TO PUSH-JERK	3	3	9	60%	25%
3	SNATCH GRIP DEADLIFT TO KNEES	3	3	9	60%	25%

Week	Exercise	Sets	Reps	Lifts	% of 1 REP MAX	Accommodating Resistance %
1	POWER SNATCH W/ OVERHEAD SQUAT	3	3	9	50%	25%
1	HANG CLEAN ABOVE KNEE	3	3	9	50%	25%
2	POWER SNATCH W/ OVERHEAD SQUAT	3	3	9	55%	25%
2	HANG CLEAN ABOVE KNEE	3	3	9	55%	25%
3	POWER SNATCH W/ OVERHEAD SQUAT	3	3	9	60%	25%
3	HANG CLEAN ABOVE KNEE	3	3	9	60%	25%

Note: "ACCOMMODATING RESISTANCE %" reflects tension at the top or finish position of the movement!

Week	Exercise	Sets	Reps	Lifts	% of 1 REP MAX	Accommodating Resistance %
1	CLEAN AND JERK	3	3	9	50%	25%
	SNATCH PULL FROM FLOOR	3	3	9	50%	25%
2	CLEAN AND JERK	3	3	9	55%	25%
	SNATCH PULL FROM FLOOR	3	3	9	55%	25%
3	CLEAN AND JERK	3	3	9	60%	25%
	SNATCH PULL FROM FLOOR	3	3	9	60%	25%

Week	Exercise	Sets	Reps	Lifts	% of 1 REP MAX	Accommodating Resistance %
1	CLEAN AND JERK	3	3	9	50%	25%
	SNATCH PULL FROM FLOOR	3	3	9	50%	25%
2	CLEAN AND JERK	3	3	9	55%	25%
	SNATCH PULL FROM FLOOR	3	3	9	55%	25%
3	CLEAN AND JERK	3	3	9	60%	25%
	SNATCH PULL FROM FLOOR	3	3	9	60%	25%

Note: "ACCOMMODATING RESISTANCE %" reflects tension at the top or finish position of the movement!

Week	Exercise	Sets	Reps	Lifts	% of 1 REP MAX	Accommodating Resistance %
1	POWER SNATCH STANDING ON BLOCK	3	3	9	50%	25%
	CLEAN PULL OFF BLOCKS	3	3	9	50%	25%
2	POWER SNATCH STANDING ON BLOCK	3	3	9	55%	25%
	CLEAN PULL OFF BLOCKS	3	3	9	55%	25%
3	POWER SNATCH STANDING ON BLOCK	3	3	9	60%	25%
	CLEAN PULL OFF BLOCKS	3	3	9	60%	25%

Note: "ACCOMMODATING RESISTANCE %" reflects tension at the top or finish position of the movement!

Week	Exercise	Sets	Reps	Lifts	% of 1 REP MAX	Accommodating Resistance %
1	POWER CLEAN W/ FRONT SQUAT	3	3	9	50%	25%
	SNATCH PULL UP TO KNEE LEVEL	3	3	9	50%	25%
2	POWER CLEAN W/ FRONT SQUAT	3	3	9	55%	25%
	SNATCH PULL UP TO KNEE LEVEL	3	3	9	55%	25%
3	POWER CLEAN W/ FRONT SQUAT	3	3	9	60%	25%
	SNATCH PULL UP TO KNEE LEVEL	3	3	9	60%	25%

- Remember a new three-week dynamic wave begins on the fourth week!

Week	Exercise	Sets	Reps	Lifts	% of 1 REP MAX	Accommodating Resistance %
1	SNATCH LEGS STRAIGHT	3	3	9	50%	25%
1	PUSH-JERK FROM STANDS	3	3	9	50%	25%
2	SNATCH LEGS STRAIGHT	3	3	9	55%	25%
2	PUSH-JERK FROM STANDS	3	3	9	55%	25%
3	SNATCH LEGS STRAIGHT	3	3	9	60%	25%
3	PUSH-JERK FROM STANDS	3	3	9	60%	25%

Note: "ACCOMMODATING RESISTANCE %" reflects tension at the top or finish position of the movement!

Week	Exercise	Sets	Reps	Lifts	% of 1 REP MAX	Accommodating Resistance %
1	POWER CLEAN FROM KNEES	3	3	9	50%	25%
1	SNATCH FROM HIGH BOX	3	3	9	50%	25%
2	POWER CLEAN FROM KNEES	3	3	9	55%	25%
2	SNATCH FROM HIGH BOX	3	3	9	55%	25%
3	POWER CLEAN FROM KNEES	3	3	9	60%	25%
3	SNATCH FROM HIGH BOX	3	3	9	60%	25%

Chapter 8: Special Notes

Chapter 8: Special Notes

It is always difficult in writing a book to know where the reader is starting from and where to stop in my own explanations. Have I given too much information or not enough? You decide and let me know. But this chapter contains special notes in many subject areas. It includes background information that may be helpful to you in understanding the process I have been through to learn what I have about strength training and weightlifting in particular. And it includes some history and some opinions.

Hopefully, you will find it of interest, and more importantly, of assistance in helping you meet your goals

Periodization

The Westside Barbell plan for periodization is a comprehensive collection of data from Soviet sports scientist's like A.S. Prilepin and his extensive research on the number of lifts per work out, plus the number of repetitions per set. This was the meager start of Westside Barbell periodization.

From 1970 to 1982 the author and everyone else used the progressive overload system, which simply means raising the bar weight each week while the repetitions were reduced as the meet approached. Unfortunately, it was based on a hypothetical number, and was, at best, a guess and not a mathematical formulation.

The first periodization system was described by Kotov in *Olympic Sport* 1917. The system separated the training into three periods:

- General
- Preparatory
- Specific

This type of training was intended for not only weight lifting. The organization of training became more precise as the years went by, not only in sports, but in sports restorations too. As Dr. Ben Tabachnik said "to adapt to training is never to fully adapt to training."

If that happened, the law of accommodation would occur. Westside found no progress after three weeks of training for any special strength and that after three weeks a detraining effect happened. It is scientifically proven that when training with an exercise for three weeks at 90 percent or greater, detraining is the result.

This led the author to a three-week pendulum wave-style training. Looking to the Soviets for guidance, the author modified the waves from Arosiev, Ermakov and other men like Vorobyev. Thus, the Westside periodization is a modified version.

The author realized that to maintain a certain max in the classical lifts a predetermined amount of volume must be maintained. It does not matter what lift you are pushing. A 400-pound squat can be maintained with 4,800 pounds of work on the squat. Every 50-pound increase requires 600 pounds of volume. Training volume is constant on week one and week three with week two having slightly raised volume in comparison. What changes each week is the percent of a one rep max without accommodating resistance. The percent for week one through week three are 75 percent to 80 percent and 85 percent on the third week returning to 75 percent on week one again to the repeat the cycle. This is done in a monthly, yearly and multi-year cycle. One must change the volume as well to avoid accommodation, while the barbell volume is set at a predetermined amount depending on your one rep max. The volume per workout is raised on the special exercises that are a 20 percent classical lifts to 80 percent special exercises ratio.

This is not new. If one wants to know the importance of this style of training you only have to look at the graph on page 79 in V.M. Zatsiorsky's book *Science and Practice of Strength Training*, Second Edition. It shows the amount of inverse curls at a certain percentage, sets and reps by Olympic champion V. Alexeev. He understood that the effects of the inverse curl were a direct effect on his snatch and clean and jerk.

Our system mirrors that system. Where one needs the most work is where Westside begins. For pulls and squats, the posterior chain is pushed to the max. Reverse hypers, inverse leg curls and back raises are done. Also, standing leg curls plus glute/ham raises—this work is very direct to the calves, hamstrings, glutes and lower back. Do power sled walking, leg presses, belt squats, hack squats on a machine and with a barbell, and also push up in not only volume, but also intensity, meaning a percent of a one rep max. The small special exercises will yield the training effect to bring forth an increase in the classical lifts as well as all special pulls and squats.

AVOID ACCOMMODATION!

Rotate a special pull or squat each workout to avoid accommodation. By keeping the percents at 75 percent to 85 percent with bar weight only or when using combination of methods training, meaning a combination of bar weight 50-60 percent plus 25 percent band tension or chain weight at lockout. The bar speed will be .8m/s to .9m/s for speed strength development. This is demonstrated by the data of A.D. Ermakov and N.S. Atanasov on page 31 of the Managing the *Training of Weightlifting* authored by N.P. Laputin and V.G. Oleshko. To master a program one must be well read, have access to unlimited special equipment and have a large number of top level lifters. Much like the Dynamo Club, who had 70 high skilled lifters, Westside has produced over 90 elite lifters.

Final Instructions

Stay with the number of lifts per workout and pay attention when doing an amount of reps per set to maintain bar speed, remember $F=ma$. Secondly on ME day, work up to a small new record in one or two lifts—mostly special pulls or squats. If your pull from below the knee goes up five pounds a month, that equals 60 pounds a year. This math equation works for any special barbell exercise or classical exercise.

Be patient and success will come to anyone.

Programming

DELAYED TRANSFORMATION

To ensure a positive result, the final phase before a contest must include a Delayed Transmutation Phase. The Westside Barbell system is a 35-day system for a double delayed transformation. Thirty-five days out, the percent on speed strength day is 85 percent for eight sets of two reps. Twenty-eight days out, the barbell weight is reduced to 75 percent for six sets of two reps. Twenty-one days out, the largest weight possible is made and new gym record is achieved (This is accomplished by doing two sets of two reps working up to three single attempts for a new record). Fourteen days out, one set of two reps then two single attempts up to 75 percent of the weight made at 21 days out. Seven days before the contest, do light special or classical lifts for two sets of two reps very light for technique. This allows for rest and adaptation resulting in a higher total.

DELAYED TRANSMUTATION

Delayed transmutation is a process of changing a group of special exercises for a certain lift. This is normally performed while not doing the lift. The Westside Barbell system never does the actual lifts, but a variety of special pulls and squats that are similar in nature to the competition lift.

An example is box squats or rack pulls off a box that is two to four inches in height. On Max Effort day, the lifts are changed each week to totally avoid accommodation. When training a particular lift for three weeks in a row, the training result will suffer if the weight is above 90 percent. However, by rotating the barbell lifts each week accommodation is avoided completely. Plus the small special exercises are rotated when necessary. Usually after three to four workouts the training results start to diminish and the small special exercises must be changed once more.

Not only must the exercises vary, but also the volume must be kept high. The high volume is 80 percent of our training with special exercises in the Westside Barbell system. It is responsible for much of the progress. This is the Conjugate System.

Not only are all exercises constantly changed, but also the volume and intensity zone. This rotation will ensure improvement of the specific motor skills. The Westside Barbell conjugate system makes it possible to raise speed, strength and raise the lifters work capacity concurrently. This makes it possible to judge all special strengths while perfecting technique as well as monitoring muscle mass gains in a weekly plan.

TRAINING SESSION

A training session or workout must be divided in a weekly plan. An extreme workout can mean high volume or high intensity. The high volume is done on speed strength day meaning the Dynamic Method, $F=ma$.

The second extreme workout is a ME day where one seeks a new TFmm (training max). Westside Barbell separates the two above workouts by 72 hours. This can be for squatting and pulling exercises with a small workout again in 10 hours. This means doing an extreme workout at 8 a.m. and a small workout comprised of small special exercises to compliment the large muscle groups trained 10 hours earlier. The same method of rest intervals applies to the pressing or jerking workouts. A small workout can be performed each day including a group of two or three exercises that will contribute to the next workout.

This requires a higher and higher level of GPP (General Physical Preparedness) and by doing this one's level of preparedness is becoming ever higher. One should never go easy on a Monday ME day to ensure making all sets powerful on speed day. By maintaining a higher volume and a gradual increase in intensity, you ensure progress along with proper restoration. A sample of a small workout can be contrasting exercises. This can speed up recovery with active rest, meaning a walk, treadmill, stair climber, med ball work or drill for flexibility and mobility. Especially for the ankle, knee, hip, lower and upper back and the shoulder.

Squats

Laputin and Oleshko dissected the most common reasons for failure in the snatch and clean and jerk on page 84 of their book *Managing the Training of Weightlifters*. Being unable to recover from the squat was only 1 percent of the failures for the snatch, but it was 15 percent of the failures in the clean and jerk. These stats were obviously taken from highly skilled weightlifters. But in the U.S., this is not the case at all.

Many men and women visit Westside Barbell who participate in weight lifting. Almost inevitably they cannot recover from their largest clean or snatch. While the stats hold true that more fail from recovering from the clean than the snatch, the percent of failure is much higher by U.S. weightlifters.

There is a misconception that one does not need a strong squat. Yet many lifters fail to recover from the squat. Or, if they do recover, they lack the ability to jerk the barbell overhead. Although constantly hearing about weightlifters squatting three times a week, after watching them they make two mistakes:

1. The squats are too light
2. The squats are too heavy.

Too light will only condition the legs and heavy effort are too slow. Like the Chinese who train the squat at 80 percent to 85 percent for eight sets of three reps or sometimes five sets of five reps controlled on the eccentric phase with the bar speed for speed strength being .8m/s, other squat workouts are for new records on ME day. This is much like the Westside System. All squats must be directed to increasing two aspects of training: Speed Development and Absolute Strength.

If you drive an everyday car or a racecar, it must shift gears at an optimal RPM. I think we can all agree on this. This is why the Westside system uses a three-week pendulum wave where two varieties are used.

The first is a 75 percent to 80 percent to 85 percent three-week wave, which as you can see increases by 5 percent each week. Then on the fourth week, will drop back to 75 percent and start over with just bar weight.

The second method is to use the combinations of Resistance Method. This system was made popular and perfected by the author (see *Supertraining* page 409). For speed strength in a three-week pendulum wave, the bar weight is 50 percent to 55 percent to 60 percent with 25 percent band tension added to the bar. The 25 percent is at lock-out in order to have good tension at the bottom of the lift. The bands not only accommodate resistance by creating over-speed eccentrics, but they add to a stronger reversal strength response. This is a virtual force effect—a force that is present, but not recognized.

Like the Chinese, Westside uses 12 sets of two reps, eight sets of three reps, or early in a training cycle, five sets of five reps to add muscle mass.

At Westside Barbell many bars are used. The standard weight lifting protocol uses back, front and overhead squats. Westside advocates overhead and front squats, but uses a wide variety of back squatting with many specialty bars.

- 14" Cambered bar
- Bow bar
- Manta ray squats
- Safety squat bar squats

We even use Zercher squats to change how the squats effect the legs and back.

BOX SQUATTING

Most squat workouts are done on a box. The box can range from a few inches above parallel to very low below parallel. Six-inch and eight-inch boxes are common. Boxes do two very important things:

1. They break up the eccentric concentric phase with a relaxed pause between switching from yielding phase to the overcoming phase.
2. The two greatest methods of strength development are static overcome by dynamic and relaxed overcome by dynamic. Box squatting when performed correctly produces both effects. One can squat much lower to a box plus much wider and lower to build unused muscles. These unused muscles hold unlimited potential for not only raising the squat, but also increasing the explosiveness part of the pull.

A special form of squatting is Belt Squatting. It can be done with a dip belt while standing on two boxes or using a belt squat machine. It is unparalleled for leg strength plus a special exercise can be performed on it by power cleaning a barbell while hanging the weight between your legs. This causes to different rates of acceleration that must be coordinated together between the legs and upper body.

An intense workout should be separated by 72 hours. Westside uses Friday for Speed Strength development and Monday for Absolute Strength development. Small workouts can be and are done every 12 hours or 24 hours. They are short 20-minute to 35-minute workouts consisting of doing GHR or Back Raises. Like the old Soviet team, 600 reps per month are done for maintenance. Other times very heavy reverse hypers and abs are done.

One must train abs like a lift, very hard and as heavy as possible. The small special exercises for the legs, hips and back are rotated as often as necessary to avoid accommodating. Just as the selection of classical lifts and special exercises and squats are constantly rotated and monitored to check progress in the classical lifts, so are the ab exercises.

After all, that is the goal: progress in speed or absolute strength. Low reps can build great strength without adding body weight. Doing high sets and reps can increase one's body weight, if that is the goal.

Equipment

To reach top form in weight lifting you must have special equipment for the development of the back and legs.

For the back and legs Westside has a list of vital pieces of special equipment.

Back
- Glute Ham Bench
- 45% Hyper Bench
- Reverse Hyper
- Good morning machine

Legs
- Plyoswing
- Belt squat
- Inverse Curl
- Hip Quad Machine
- Standing leg curl

Bodybuilders and powerlifters have developed many machines and bars to improve the physique and strength. The weightlifter must follow their example. The Soviet team was doing many of the above exercises and using apparatuses like belt squats, Goodmorning machine, non-motorized treadmills and pulling heavy sleds and they made use of specialty bars as well. They also used boxes for jumping onto and off in order to build explosive power and absolute strength for depth jumps. Westside has developed 75 men over 800 pounds in the squat, 22 over 1,000 pounds and two over 1,200 pounds. Westside lifter Dave Hoff's 1,210 pounds at 271-pound bodyweight is the greatest coefficient squat recorded.

Hoff's teammate Laura Phelps Sweatt has the women's greatest coefficient squat of 775 pounds at

165 pounds. This is not a coincidence, but rather a well thought out system. The rotation of large and small exercises is the basis of the Westside conjugate system. This system was first tested at the world famous Dynamo Club in the former Soviet Union. It started with 25 to 40 special exercises and grew to at least 100 specially designed workouts with the barbell only, not counting the small special exercises like GHR and back raises, Kettlebell work and the list goes on. This was to find weaknesses, raise technique and build greater GPP for recovery.

There is **NO EXCUSE** not to acquire some of the above mentioned equipment, or better yet all, if you want to excel. A bodybuilding gym is well equipped with many devices to increase muscle mass. A powerlifting gym is equally equipped with anything that possibly could help increase strength.

One goal of the Conjugate System is to develop a weak muscle group to increase technique. We all have great technique with light weight, but once the weight grows to our physical limits strange things happen.

The back rounds. It can't stand up after the clean or it fails to jerk the weight over the head.

What happened to that flawless technique? It became not so flawless. Why? A weak muscle group will show its ugly face when the bar grows heavy.

To reach an advanced stage you must employ a wide variety of special means. This includes many bars and special machines to develop a particular muscle group. Very few are biomechanically perfect to build lifts. This is why almost everyone must do small special exercises for the low or upper back, hamstrings, glutes, quads, abs, and even calves. Just one lacking muscle groups can spell complete failure in one phase of the lift. The author started Westside Barbell with a power rack, a hyperextension bench, a flat bench plus a bar and weights.

First, more weights were needed. Then, a safety squat bar. Now, present day, we have every conceivable bar and machine from an Isokinetic machine, electric stimulation to the specialized machines that are patented and trademarked to advance any athlete to the top. If you follow the same course you will find the same results.

Weightlifting Methods of Those Strongest

Here is an overview at the different methods I have studied.

THE CHINESE METHOD

It is quite easy to recognize the influence of the former Soviet Union training methods while watching the Chinese coaches set forth their training methods. Their weightlifting pool came mostly from young kids in rural areas. Many Chinese youths participated in sports, like American kids do, ranging from soccer, swimming, Ping-Pong, basketball and baseball.

But there are many who want to leave the country life and possibly make a living on the weightlifting platform.

There is great pressure to excel. But unlike the Bulgarian system, there is room for the weightlifter to help form his or her training regimen to some extent. The coach will stress perfect lifting technique not only in the classical lifts, but also in the special pulls as well as how to front and back squat. The emphasis is back squatting over front squatting, and squats are mostly very heavy and performed usually twice a week.

They feel most progress is based on the back squat. They squat with feet at least shoulder width apart and push for the new records. They lower themselves into a squat—not just dropping and trying to bounce back up, nor do they squat so low as to let the lower back loosen up. "Use your back, not just the legs," the coach advises his lifters. Goodmornings, standing and seated, glute ham raises, and back raises are special assistance for squatting as well as pulling.

When performing squats for a workout, they do a large volume at 80 percent to 85 percent. The number of lifts can range from 24 lifts to 40 lifts. A.S. Priplin's charts indicated no more than 20 lifts at the 80 percent zone with four reps the most per set. So it is easy to understand how much emphasis the Chinese place on squatting sometimes as many as five reps per set.

As far as general training plans are organized. The lifter helps plan their exercises to some extent. The same holds true in the style of jerk they will utilize namely power, split or squat jerk. Remember, their front squat must be at least 15 percent greater than their clean! The coach always emphasizes the importance of the back strength and tightens.

The special exercises consist of, not only work for the spinal erectors, but the abs as well using such exercises as:

- Leg raises
- Side bends,
- Planks facing up and down

They do lots of GPP on each workout and end with some hypertrophy or bodybuilding style sets such as:

- Tricep extensions
- Dips
- Push-ups, etc.

The bodybuilding is done at the end of the workout. A few sets to near or total failure usually up to six sets. The Chinese place great stress on the lats and upper back development. Thinking about their program and doing overhead presses reminds me to encourage you to remember to use a belt and wrists wraps when fatiguing the lower back or wrists. The upper body must be strong for the jerk or you will fail to reach your absolute potential in that phase of the lift as well as the snatch and the clean. I have talked about the other important muscle groups earlier.

It also brings to mind these two thoughts about increasing the clean and jerk:

- Build stronger legs for pulling and recovering from a low position. For pushing up the jerk, do one clean and two jerks per set. The hips must play a large role in the second pull to fully extend your hips and knees.
- For clean pulls, work up to failure on most workouts. They work up to a weight until their back is rounded—sometimes to the point they can't lift the bar off the platform. But if you manage to clear the floor pull until you stand up regardless if the back rounds or not.

When talking about special strengths from speed strength to strength speed to absolute strength, the coach says, "speed and strength are important, but strength is the limiting factor on success." Beginners must focus on Absolute strength for years. To the point, many elite weightlifters must continue to raise their top strength. This calls for breaking records by doing max singles. One can lift a larger weight for one rep then two or three reps and, of course, in competition you lift one rep per attempt. One must also train the mind to do this and this is for the lifter to do.

A coach can only program and focus on technique. "Train your weakness" their coach advices. They use many styles of squatting such as:

- Front
- Back
- Rack Squats off pins
- Pause squats
- Concentric squats.

OTHER NOTES ON TECHNIQUE

The Chinese Coach says to "lean slightly forward when front squatting, causing the back muscles to play their role, which is large." If training is extremely heavy for two weeks there would be 72 hours between the next workouts. Or do two workouts much lighter in not only intensity, but also volume. Like the special notes on Bulgarian Methods this is just a small sample of the Chinese training methods.

They too have excellent coaches at different age groups starting as young as eight years old.

THE SOVIET METHOD

The Soviet weight lifting system was a well thought through process. They first watched all the greatest lifters from other countries to obtain valuable data on which to base their training system.

There are too many sports scientists to name, but I.P. Zhekov's book of biomechanics of their weightlifting exercises is one who must be mentioned. The foundation of their system arrived from men like Iluchkin, V.I. Frolov, S.I. Lelikov, and many more gave insight to Zhekov's concepts. Later Y.V. Verkhoshansky, A.S. Medvedyev, R.A. Roman plus V.I. Zatsiorsky and others were the author's inspiration to solve the riddle of the Soviet Union system.

The conjugate system was a special project by men like Y.V. Verkhoshansky with the assistance of 70 highly qualified weightlifters at the world famous Dynamo Club. It was first introduced with a rotation of 25 to 40 special and classical exercises. After this experiment, only one lifter was satisfied leaving the others wanting more exercises. This led to A.S. Medvedyev to use at least 100 different weightlifting exercises for a multi-year program.

Like the Chinese, the Soviet system was designed to build a weightlifter over a long period. This process would start at 11-years-old with every two years graduating to a higher level of perfection until one would hopefully step on the world stage at 19- to 21-years-old. The system comprised of many special exercises to bring forth the weak areas of the body to perfect form and to raise speed and absolute strength. This came in many applications of pulling, such as using four positions to start the pull itself, but also to prolong leg drive.

Some snatches were done with a closer grip at times as well as doing clean pulls and cleans with a wide grip, some with legs straight as well as muscle up snatches and cleans. Small exercises were employed such as rows of all variety. Chins and, of course, back raises, GHD, Goodmornings, both seated and standing, were all used to aid in GPP—General Physical Preparedness. Of course, this is just a small list. V. Alexis would do 1,000 steps in a pool to increase his abs and hip strength and has been known to do 100 power snatches with 100 kg in some low intensity workouts.

It was common to see Soviet weightlifters duck walking and lunging as part of their preparation for the heavy squats and pulls. Heavy squats were a large part of the program much like the Chinese program. Back squats, front squats and starting in the bottom position concentrically were the order of things.

While the Bulgarian team would attempt near maxes constantly pushing as close to 100 percent of their best based on a daily max in the snatch, clean and jerk, the Soviet team would work up to All-Time Records in the special exercises and squats over a 50 percent ratio after achieving a "Master of Sport" status.

Roughly 50 percent of the snatches, cleans and jerks were performed at 75 percent to 85 percent, which is very similar to the Chinese system. According to the data by A.D. Ermakov and N.S. Atanasov, 16 percent of the snatches were done at 90 percent and 8 percent at 95 percent leaving 2.5 percent at 100 percent. They relied on max effort work in the pulls and squats for the classical lifts to avoid accommodation.

They brought forth strength in the weakest muscle groups by performing large special exercises—meaning pulls and squats—and small special exercises, referring to back raises, GHR, jumps and abs. Loading was the priority for the Russians in the amount of reps and total lifts in one workout. A.S. Prilepin's' data was at the forefront of their training design. The key word was OPTIMAL in their reps and lifts of a certain percent to control volume and bar speed. This was their key to constant progress.

Unfortunately, there was so much data from many coaches from large institutes to small city gyms that it was not all discussed with other teams. Thus, not all of their vast knowledge is known. Special exercises were very important to their system to the point that the amount of inverse curls performed during a training cycle were as many as 600 per month for maintenance.

V. Alexeev used a three-week pendulum wave. This made it possible to monitor his training in a short-term plan.

1. The Maximal Effort Method, meaning lifting a weight limited to one rep, is superior to all others methods.
2. The Dynamic Effort Method is for increasing a fast rate of force development.
3. The Repetition Method is lifting a sub maximal weight to near or total failure.

The Soviets developed and used these methods and used them for the development of all velocities: low velocity for strength speed, intermediate velocity for speed strength and fast velocity for explosive strength. They truly perfected sports science by employing sports science to regulate the training of weightlifting and track and field. They realized that without this combined effort, it was impossible to reach the international stage.

In 1964, the coach could not understand why their only champion, Leonid Zhabotinsky, was not making progress after the Olympics. They studied his training data and found that he had made no progress in two years. Finding his training intensity had decreased they had to push up the intensity and in 1967, once again, his total started to increase.

A key to their progress was also in restoration methods. They realized the way to train harder was also tied to recovery. You may find many similarities to the Soviet and Chinese training methodologies. Both systems have a longer success rate for a lifter to be on a world stage for many years.

THE BULGARIAN METHOD

The Bulgarian's main theory was to enlist young men 11- to 13-years-old who could learn to lift near maximal weights. A lot of this thinking was by Soviet sports scientists like Fomin and others. In addition, all lifters must be perfectly proportioned for their weight class.

The coach relied on a limited amount for exercises to excel, not on GPP, which is contradictory to the Soviet, Chinese and, of course, the Westside System. You may look at Nam's very successful career, but he was a perfect lifting machine.

Are You? I doubt it!

They knew the Maximum Effort Method was superior to all other methods. When looking at Nam's training weekly program in 1980 his average training intensity was 77 percent combining classical and special lifts, but by 1981 it was raised to 85 percent combing classical and special lifts.

At a bodyweight of 52 kg his total was 250 kg in 1982. It rose to 290 kg at 56 kg in 1983. Then after moving up to 60 kg, his best year was 1988 in Seoul with 342.5 kg. For the most part, the routine below is what one undertook as a Bulgarian weightlifter.

For the standard exercises special and classical were:
- Snatch from stands about knee height
- Jerk from stands
- Front and back squats
- Snatch Pull

Nam's best total coincides with his largest training volume. This is what Westside's principle is, but with the exception of a 20 percent to 80 percent ratio of classical to special exercises. Westside strongly believes Nam's technique is nearly perfect due to his perfect proportions.

Westside has held Nam in high esteem both then and now. The author has seen many athletes who have a million dollar body, but with a 10 cent mind. Nam, thankfully, had it all both physically and mentally, which made him one of the greatest along with many of his teammates. The Bulgarian system basically was to do circa maximal training all year long. They used no exceptionally heavy squats due to constantly raising from near limit snatch and cleans and jerks.

A major point of interest was their selection of a weightlifter. Could they handle the stress on the body? Could they handle the mental stress of a six-day-a-week program when they are asked to do all-time or near-maximal lifts every workout. And last, but certainly not least, full access to advanced restoration methods and three good meals a day plus financial support.

A high percentage would not hold up to the demands, truly "Only the Strong Would Survive"!

The junior athletes trained at the same facility as the senior team members and under one set of coaches. The Bulgarian training system was one-dimensional and if you could not adapt to a very singular method you were "excused" from the program. Only model weightlifters with strong mental qualities could exist. There is a wide uncertainty in the amount of maximum lifts. The Bulgarians performed in a yearly plan that could add up to 4,000 lifts, which included special or classical lifts. The Russian system accounted for about 600 lifts in comparison to this. The Bulgarian plan was based on daily maximums not an All-Time Records, and this accounts for the 4,000 lifts. The Soviet plan only counted an All-Time Record in a special squat, pull or two classical lifts.

All the weightlifters were subjected to psychological, anatomical and physiological testing to improve their chances of success. Ivan Abadjiev, the renowned Bulgarian Weightlifting Federation coach from 1968 to 1989 and again from 1997 to 2000, truly believed in the Law of Adaptation and used very young lifters who could lift near limit weights all the time to raise the average percent of their one rep maximum. This had great success, but also came at a great price as too many young men could not cope with the stress of constant training and high-level competition.

The Westside System

The author used his analytical mind to choose the best of all three systems to form the Westside system.

What is an Analytical Mind, and how do you use it?

Analytical thinking is a critical component of visual thinking that gives one an ability to solve problems quickly and effectively. It involves the process of gathering relevant information and identifying key issues related to this information. It requires you to compare sets of data from different sources; identify cause and effect patterns; and draw appropriate conclusions to arrive at appropriate solutions.

The author quotes Albert Einstein when he says you can win an argument with intelligent men, but you will never win an argument with ignorant men. So I hope the reader has an open, intelligent mind and a commitment to follow the Westside system as it was developed through scientific models and practical experience.

Westside Barbell has two Maximal Effort Days separated by 72 hours and two Speed Strength days also separated by 72 hours as well as at least four small workouts per weekly plan. A ratio of 20 percent of barbell squats and deadlifts are done a week with 80 percent special exercises both small and large and this comprises the bulk of the training. All squats are on a box and no straight weight deadlifts off the floor are done. Instead, we use special means deadlifts standing on a box or with the weight placed upon a box or rack pins using a variety of stances for both squats and pulls.

Westside Barbell has 22 over 1,000 pound squatters with 198 pounds being the lightest lifter to squat this weight. We have more than 22 men over 800 pounds in the deadlift with two lifters over 900 pounds and a top five average of 880 pounds.

Westside is also home to the best coefficient man and woman lifters of All-Time, plus has the largest total of 3,005 pounds at 271-pound bodyweight. As of this writing, five women out of 10 weight classes and two men out of 12 weight classes hold All-Time Total Records.

For periodization, a monthly plan consists of 80 lifts for speed strength squats and 40 lifts for speed strength deadlifts. For Maximum Effort, the numbers are four minimal lifts, seven optimal lifts and 10 maximal lifts. After moving to 90 percent of a one rep maximum, two more attempts are performed ending with an All-Time record. A monthly plan consists of 12 lifts at 90 percent to 100 percent plus.

After all, there are three attempts in a contest!

Two exercises can be done in one workout with a 20-minute break between lifts. An example would be two pulls—one below the knee, the second on the top of the leg—or a front squat and then an overhead press. Westside totally relies on the data of men like A.S. Prilepin and A.D. Ermakov and N.S. Atanasov as well as Y.I. Frolov's work for choosing the weight for the classical lifts and special pulls.

The Conjugate System is in constant use for the rotation of special exercises plus intensity zones and volumes. It goes much further by relying on Special Bars to squat and press with.

Many records are broken at over 90 percent rate for the 20 odd lifters at Westside's private facility. While not owning a college degree, the author has 10 U.S patents for a low back machine, hamstring machine and a static dynamic developer. He has been a Top 10 lifter for 30 years, covering five decades and holding USPF elite status for 37 years while using the Soviet System for a power lifting team that dominates their rivals. The system is now prepared for the sport for which it was intended–weightlifting—by combining the best of all three systems.

The author suggests you use slightly less volume and five percent lower intensity for the classical lifts due to the lack of GPP.

Also, there is a lack of leg strength throughout American weightlifting. This must be addressed if we ever expect to excel in weightlifting. But we must first build a base to choose from, starting with 10-year-olds. This would allow 10-year-olds to truly master their art. The US has failed to establish itself on the international stage.

We also must look elsewhere for the answer to improving our nation's lifters. But where? The answer is right in front of us! The two logical systems are from China and Russia, both countries that build the lifter. This book offers a plan for anyone who has mastered technique, but lacks strength. It is simplistic in its approach with the loading of volume and correct intensities, GPP and the rotation of classical and special exercises.

Recruiting

When recruiting a lifter or a coach, try to avoid an introvert. Introvert means turning inward or folding inward. A person who is introverted tends to do better on their own and they do not need extra external stimuli for their own fulfillment. My observation of weightlifting in the USA is that it has become introverted. This MUST stop, as the walls have closed up on it with no easy way out.

On the other hand, an extrovert is someone who looks outside or beyond to gain friends and teammates while solving problems. Look for an extrovert to coach you or to lift for you.

An extrovert coach will find new methods to raise your status as a lifter. Extrovert coaches are always seeking advice from others with greater knowledge of speed, strength and technique–whatever it takes to put one of his or her lifters on the top podium. The coach must pick a lifter that is first built for weight lifting, but most of all mentally and emotionally stable enough to reach the top of the sport. I don't mean only the US stage, but the WORLD stage. It takes many programs to choose from and rotate in a weekly, monthly, yearly and multi-year plan. A wide variety of special equipment must be available to bring up weak muscle groups. I hear constantly how we cannot compete with the Chinese or the Russians, but this is just an excuse. Committing to change will make a difference in our results.

Our colleges recruit sprinters from one part of a country and long distance sprinters from another such as Jamaica and Africa. America once owned Pro Boxing, but Russians are the undisputed champions at heavyweight, light heavyweight and Triple G at middleweight. Only Klitcho lives outside the USA. There are other Lightweight fighters who hold world belts in boxing who are also from Russia, but live in the USA.

These recruitment practices hold true for our soccer and baseball teams as well. What's the point? The point is that if you believe the Chinese and Russians are better at lifting, then there is a large population of Chinese and Russian people in the USA, so why not try to enlist them, not only to lift, but to coach. Westside Barbell is a private gym in Columbus, Ohio, and 80 percent of our lifters are from either out of state or out of this country from places such as Russia, Sweden, and Finland to name a few. If you think an ethnic group holds the answer, then go recruit that ethnic group within the US. Please follow the lead of other sports that have a place on the world stage. This can be done if you think outside the box. Start with a 10- to 12-year-old group, then junior high school that will lead later to high school varsity and finally a college scholarship. Recruited young people will likely need much better coaching.

Don't wait until the chosen one walks into your gym, but find him or her before they are involved in a different sport.

Chapter 9: Special Exercises For Strength Development

Chapter 9: Special Exercises For Strength Development

Box Squats

Why box squat if you are a weightlifter? Simple—using an assortment of box heights such as the high box that could range from 17 inches to 20 inches can be used to overload the squat. This can greatly help the leg drive or thrust phase in the jerk. Front or back squats can be done as well. Use strictly below-parallel squats on speed day for acceleration for the recovery of the snatch or clean. Very low squats can be done on a 10-inch, 8-inch or even a 6-inch box for recovering from a deep clean or snatch.

BACK TO THE QUESTION—WHY BOX SQUATS?

A box squat is the greatest special exercise for the regular squat. You are able to use a very low box. Jon Stafford at six feet would use an 8-inch box for starting strength for the deadlift. His pull is 832 pounds at 275-pounds bodyweight. Stafford could not squat 8-inch off the platform in the regular squat, but by releasing the hip muscles it made it possible to not only touch the box, but fully relax the hips. By reflexing the hips, glutes, and hamstrings, you can explode concentrically to lockout. This is the key to box squatting: releasing the muscles and reflexing them. While weightlifters can squat very deep, they can't lower themselves in the deep eccentric phase nor can they use a wide stance and squat deep. By squatting one way all the time, some critical muscles are disregarded completely. The squat is limited as well as the hips, glutes, and hamstrings that contribute to pulling strength. The weightlifter has not only limited his strength potential, but also his flexibility.

Two of the greatest methods to build absolute and explosive strength are 1) static overcome by dynamic and 2) relaxed overcome by dynamic. Box squats do both simultaneously if done correctly.

WHAT IS CORRECT BOX SQUATTING?

By lowering onto the box, one must sit back using posterior chain. After sitting fully on the box with the back arched, knees push out to the side to fully activate the hips. While on the box, release the hips and glutes while keeping everything else completely tight. By doing this you will flex off the box very explosively to the top. The greater the explosive strength, the greater the distance you separate yourself from the box initially.

Box squats use all the muscles dramatically that are not heavily used while doing regular squats. The weightlifter has well-conditioned legs, but weak hips. Box squats will alone increase your pulls with a new-found strength. Box squats are a part of the puzzle, don't neglect them!

Accommodating Resistance

The reason to use accommodating resistance is to develop maximal tension throughout the entire lift or range of motion. This is superior to working at only the weakest point of the lift. This is not a new method of training as it was introduced by Zander in 1879.

One method of accommodating resistance is isokinetic – this is where a machine is used at a constant speed set before exercising and kept constant regardless of the amount of force applied by the lifter.

A second is made possible by a Nautilus-style machine with its odd-shaped cam.

A third method, stated in Supertraining by Dr. Mel Siff (2004 sixth edition) made popular by the author is a combination of resistance methods where chains and rubber bands are used on the barbell. This method is also discussed in Science and Practice of Strength Training by V.M Zatsiorsky (Second Edition).

COMBINING RESISTANCE METHODS

First, chains were applied to the bar in the early '90s. After experimenting for 18 months and three major meets, it was determined they were very useful for Compensatory Acceleration Training (CAT) made popular by Dr. Fred Hatfield. The CAT system was used to eliminate bar deceleration, but it was impossible to fully eliminate bar deceleration with bar weight only on less than maximal loads.

The author solved the problem completely by using chains on the bars. Dave Williams, the head strength coach at Liberty University, called the author and asked me to do experiments with jump stretch bands. The rest is strength history!

The band made it possible to duplicate CAT, but added a bonus—over speed eccentrics, which caused a tremendous stretch reflex. Twenty-five percent band tension at lockout works for speed strength, or the faster down the faster up. This is basic physics. For the development of strength speed/slow strength, use 50 percent of the total load at the top, which consists of band tension with this method. Example: a 600-pound squatter would use 300 pounds of band tension at the top plus bar weight. This would be a form of shock training. By using over-speed eccentrics, it provides involuntary or passive acceleration. When doing depth jumps, a body falling through space at 9.8 m/s provides KE (kinetic energy) while landing on a surface. When using rubber bands, the force is generated by external elastic tension. The system of using band tension on the eccentric phase is referred to as Accelerated Powermetrics.

Bands can be used for squats, Goodmornings, pressing, pulling, all at different positions. For pulls in hang position, position can be done in two ways: Accelerated Eccentric or Accelerated Ballistic training. Remember to start with light band tension measured at the top of the lift. Note: Tension must be on the bar at the start of the lift to eliminate momentum. This training can be hard on the lifter, after all, this is supramaximal force training. It is always important to increase acceleration and then mass. More can be found on the subject in two of the books previously mentioned: Supertraining and Science and Practice of Strength Training.

Bands

Bands can be the key to decrease errors in technique—many times the snatch is missed due to incomplete extension of the torso during the explosion. After training with the correct band tension, you learn to fully pull through with the barbell to the highest point.

MISGUIDING THE BARBELL TRAJECTORY

This means the falling forward or backwards. After fixing weights overhead while using bands in the jerk, pressing, or overhead squat, your stabilizers will have grown accustomed to holding the barbell strongly. The two errors mentioned above account for 91 percent of all missed snatches.

For the jerk, again fixing the barbell correctly overhead is the most common reason to fail in a competition.

LEG STRENGTH

The next reason for failure has to do with lack of leg strength:

First—not working legs maximally during the jerk.

Second—inability to recover from the squat. Thirty-six percent of all missed attempts account for this. By squatting with bands on front, back, and overhead squats on speed strength day it causes one to extend legs fully and powerfully at the top. Also, to recover from cleans and power cleans, do half and one-fourth squats with maximal acceleration. This is greatly lacking in squat training.

SPEED STRENGTH WORKOUT

The speed strength squat workout will be explained in detail below. It is based on our top squat with most workouts using 50 percent week one, 55 percent week two, and 60 percent week three with 25 percent band tension at lockout. Add some waves with 75 percent week one, 80 percent week two, and 85 percent week three with bar weight plus a small amount of chain. Most will be on a box.

While others regular squat, add front and overhead squat. Remember to use a percent of a particular squat.

EXAMPLES

- 25 percent band tension front squat with a max of 500 pounds
    - 50 percent 250 pounds
    - 55 percent 275 pounds
    - 60 percent 300 pounds
- 25 percent band tension back squat with a max of 600 pounds
    - 50 percent 300 pounds
    - 55 percent 330 pounds
    - 60 percent 360 pounds
- 25% band tension overhead squat with a max of 400 pounds
    - 50 percent 200 pounds
    - 55 percent 220 pounds
    - 60 percent 240 pounds

Over speed eccentrics will aid in the time to squat under the bar. Two of the fastest under the bar were Dave Rigert and Yuri Vardanyan who broke numerous records for the former Soviet team. Because the bands are pulling down on the bar, you the lifter have no choice than to pull one's self under the bar much quicker than with a regular bar.

Example: Imagine dropping a rock to the ground versus shooting a rock to the ground with a sling shot. Get the picture?

To master weightlifting, first perfect form, then, develop special strength.

1) Plus maximum strength—use all muscles involved during the lift. Fmm

2) Starting strength—here one must develop force at the beginning of the muscle contractions before the barbell movement occurs.

3) Acceleration Strength—this means to have the ability over time to quickly achieve maximal external force while developing muscle tension at the beginning of a dynamic contraction.

Note: Bands develop a fast rate of force—for more information read *Supertraining* sixth edition 2003 by Dr. Mel Siff.

Remember that speed of movement is determined on maximum muscular strength. This is where the men are separated from the boys (see Hill's equation of muscle contraction also in *Supertraining*.)

Exercise Illustrations
Large Exercises

Bent Over Row - A

Bent Over Row - B

Bow Bar Squat

Cambered Bar Squat

Clean Pull Standing on Mat

Clean - A

Clean - B

Clean - C

Clean - D

Clean and Split Jerk - A

Clean and Split Jerk - B

Clean and Split Jerk - C

Clean and Split Jerk - D

Clean and Split Jerk - E

Clean and Split Jerk - F

Snatch - A

Snatch - B

Snatch - C

Snatch - D

Snatch - E

Muscle Snatch - A

Muscle Snatch - B

Muscle Snatch - C

Muscle Snatch - D

Clean and Press Against Mini Bands (Single Strand) - A

Clean and Press Against Mini Bands (Single Strand) - B

137

Clean and Press Against Mini Bands (Single Strand) - C

Clean and Press Against Mini Bands (Single Strand) - D

Clean and Press Against Mini Bands (Single Strand) - E

Clean and Press Against Mini Bands (Single Strand) - F

Goodmornings with Safety Bar - A

Goodmornings with Safety Bar - B

Goodmornings with Safety Bar and Bands - A

144

Goodmornings with Safety Bar and Bands - B

Back Squat - A

Back Squat - B

Overhead Squat - A

Overhead Squat - B

Overhead Squat - C

Overhead Squat - D

Low Box Squat with Safety Squat Bar - A

Low Box Squat with Safety Squat Bar - B

Manta Ray - Start - A

Manta Ray - B

Clean from a 4-inch Box - A

Clean from a 4-inch Box - B

Clean from a 4-inch Box - C

Clean from a 4-inch Box - D

Snatch from a 4-inch Box - A

Snatch from a 4-inch Box - B

Snatch from a 4-inch Box - C

Snatch from a 4-inch Box - D

Snatch from a 4-inch Box - E

Snatch from a 4-inch Box - F

Close Grip Snatch From a 4-inch Box - A

Close Grip Snatch From a 4-inch Box - B

Close Grip Snatch From a 4-inch Box - C

Close Grip Snatch From a 4-inch Box - D

Close Grip Snatch From a 4-inch Box - E

Close Grip Snatch From a 4-inch Box - F

Concentric Squat - A

Concentric Squat - B

Concentric Squat - C

Concentric Squat - D

High Box Squat Into Overhead Press From Rack - A

High Box Squat Into Overhead Press From Rack - B

High Box Squat Into Overhead Press From Rack - C

High Box Squat Into Overhead Press From Rack - D

High Box Squat Into Overhead Press From Rack - E

High Box Squat Into Overhead Press From Rack - F

Split Jerk from Pins - A

Split Jerk from Pins - B

Split Jerk from Pins - C

Split Jerk from Pins - D

Russian Twists - A

Russian Twists - B

Russian Twists - C

Russian Twists - D

Russian Twists - E

Russian Twists - F

High Pulls Narrow Grip - A

High Pulls Narrow Grip - B

High Pulls Narrow Grip - C

High Pulls Wide Grip - A

High Pulls Wide Grip - B

High Pulls Wide Grip - C

High Pulls Wide Grip - D

Power Snatch With Overhead Squat - A

Power Snatch With Overhead Squat - B

Power Snatch With Overhead Squat - C

Power Snatch With Overhead Squat - D

Safety Bar Squat - A

Safety Bar Squat - B

Shrugs Regular Grip - A

Shrugs Regular Grip - B

Shrugs Wide Grip - A

Shrugs Wide Grip - B

Single-Hand Deadlift - A

Single-Hand Deadlift - B

Single-Handed Snatch - A

Single-Handed Snatch - B

Single-Handed Snatch - C

Single-Handed Snatch - D

Snatch from Box with Overhead Squat - A

Snatch from Box with Overhead Squat - B

Snatch from Box with Overhead Squat - C

Snatch from Box with Overhead Squat - D

Push Press Plus Jerk from a Box - A

Push Press Plus Jerk from a Box - B

Push Press Plus Jerk from a Box - C

Push Press Plus Jerk from a Box - D

Snatch for the Hang Position - A

Snatch for the Hang Position - B

Snatch for the Hang Position - C

Front Squat Into an Overheard Press - A

Front Squat Into an Overheard Press - B

Static Squats - A

Static Squats - B

Static Lunge Performed on the Westside Barbell Static/Dynamic Machine

Static Front Squat Performed on the Westside Barbell Static/Dynamic Machine (see picture right page 215)

Static Squat Performed on the Westside Barbell Static/Dynamic Machine

Straight Leg Deadlift - A

216

Straight Leg Deadlift - B

Straight Leg Deadlift - C

Upright Row - A

Upright Row - B

Upright Row - C

Zercher Squat - A

Zercher Squat - B

Zercher Squat - C

Zercher Squat - D

Zercher Squat - E

General Physcial Prepardness
GPP

General Physical Preparedness (GPP) Sled - A

GPP Walking with a Safety Squat Bar - B

GPP Walking with a Safety Squat Bar - A

GPP Walking with a Safety Squat Bar - B

GPP Walking with a Weight Vest - A

GPP Walking with a Weight Vest - B

GPP Wheel Barrow - A

GPP Wheel Barrow - B

GPP Wheel Barrow (Rickshaw)- A

GPP Wheel Barrow (Rickshaw)- B

GPP Yoke Walk - A

GPP Yoke Walk - B

Exercise Illustrations
Small Exercises

Banded Hamstring Curls - A

Banded Hamstring Curls - B

Banded Hamstring Curls - C

Banded Hamstring Curls - D

Barbell Twists - A

Barbell Twists - B

Barbell Twists - C

Barbell Twists - D

Belt Squat Exercises - Walk

Decline Bench Sit Ups - A

Decline Bench Sit Ups - B

252

Decline Bench Sit Ups - C

Decline Bench Sit Ups - D

253

Depth Jumps - A

Depth Jumps - B

Depth Jumps - C

Depth Jumps - D

Seated Box Jumps - A

Seated Box Jumps - B

Seated Box Jumps - C

Seated Box Jumps - D

Seated Box Jumps - E

Standing Box Jumps - A

Standing Box Jumps - B

Standing Box Jumps - C

Standing Box Jumps - D

Dips - A

Dips - B

Dips - C

Dips - D

Glute Ham Back Extension With Sandbag - A

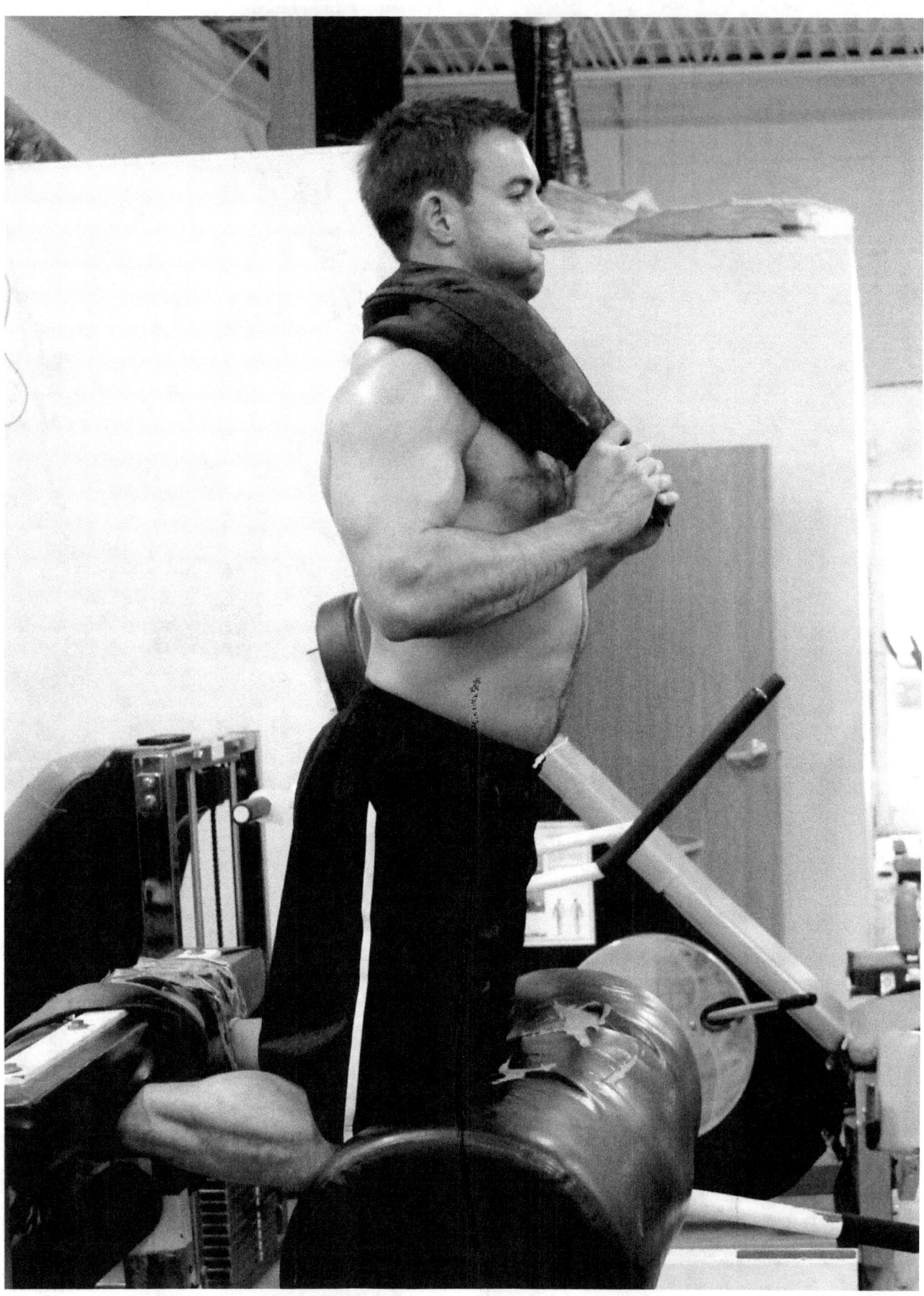

Glute Ham Back Extension With Sandbag - B

Glute Ham Back Extension With Sandbag - C

Glute Ham Back Extension With Sandbag - D

Inverse Curl - A

Inverse Curl - B

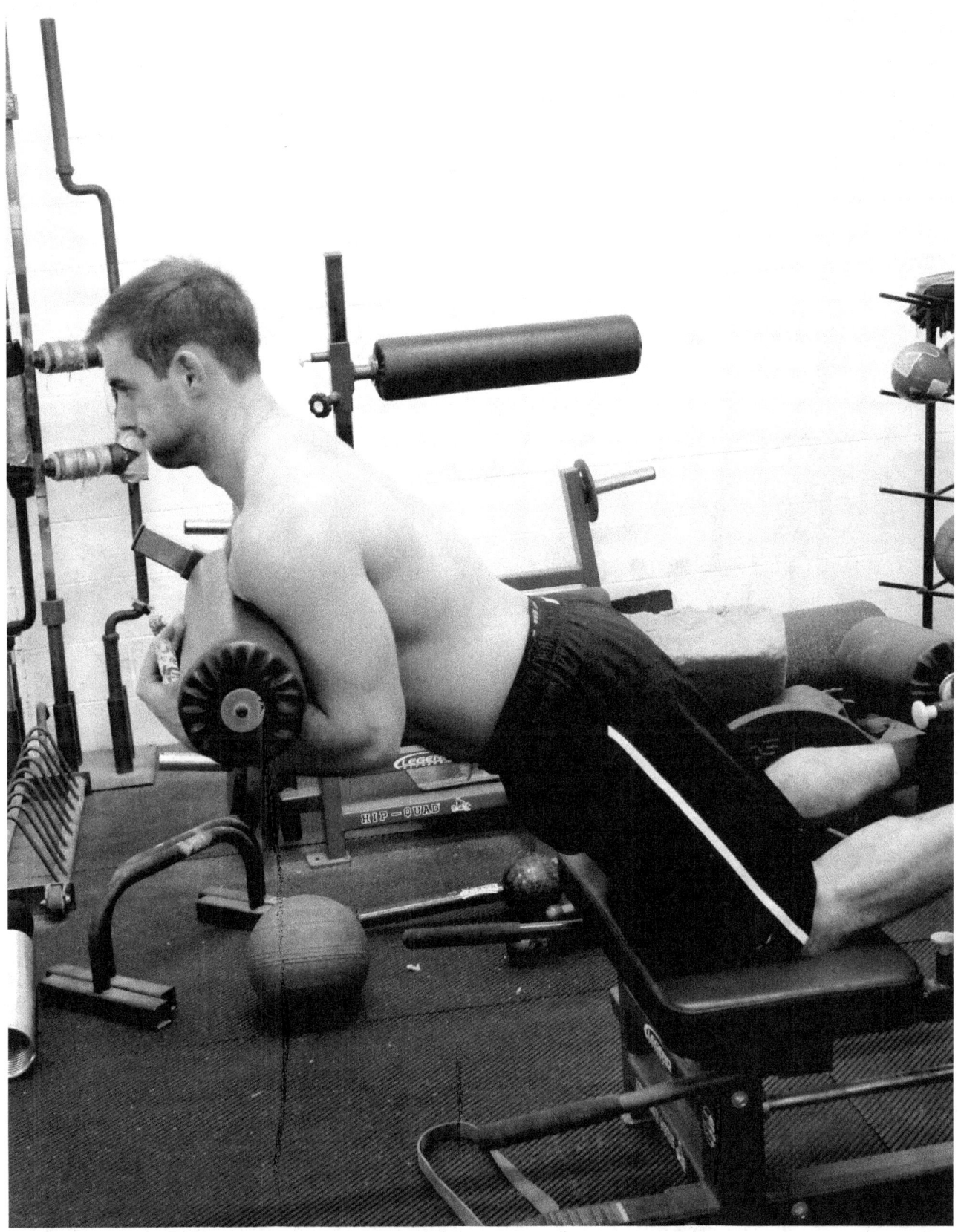

Inverse Curl - C

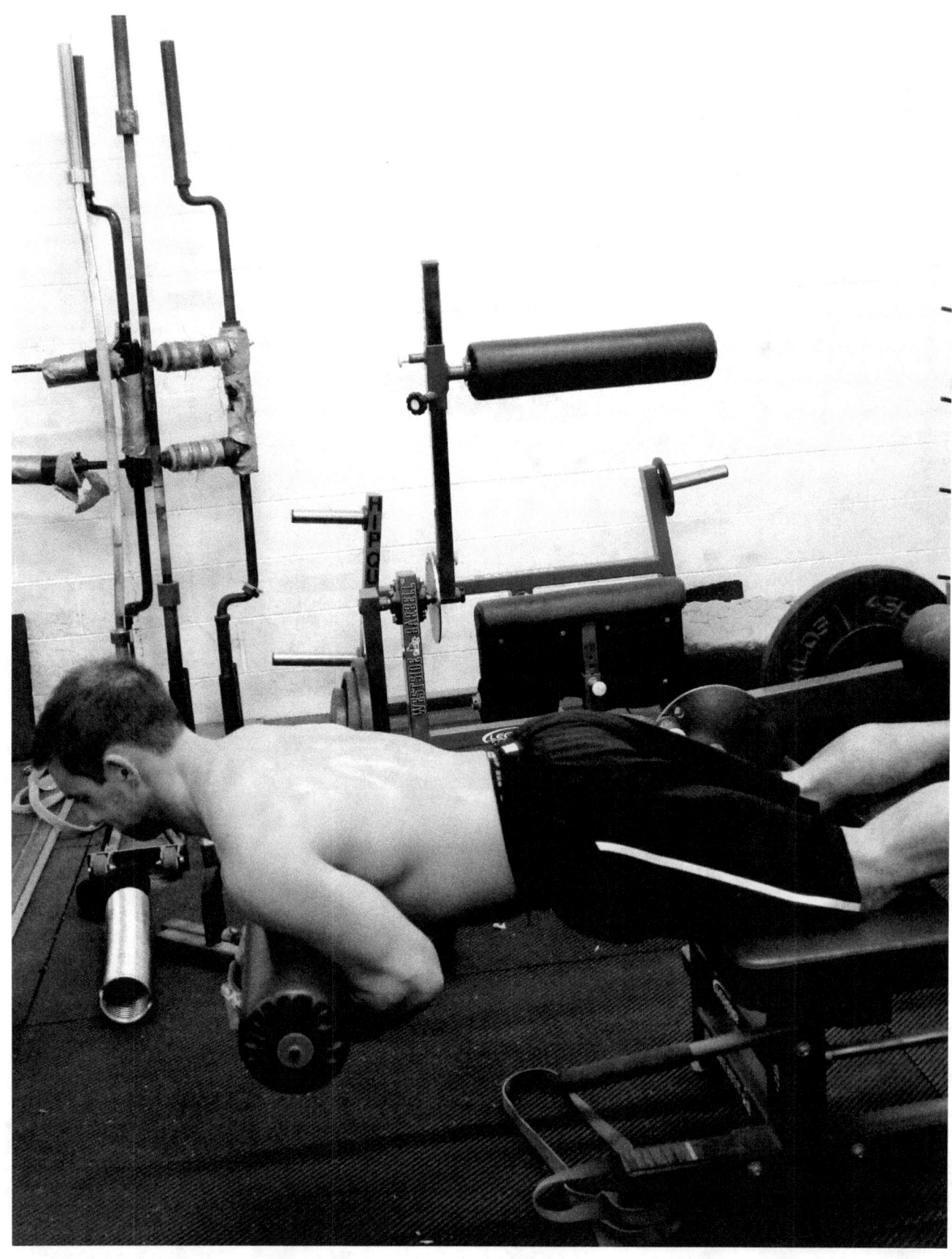

Inverse Curl - D

Inverse Curl - E

Inverse Curl - F

Belt Squats - A

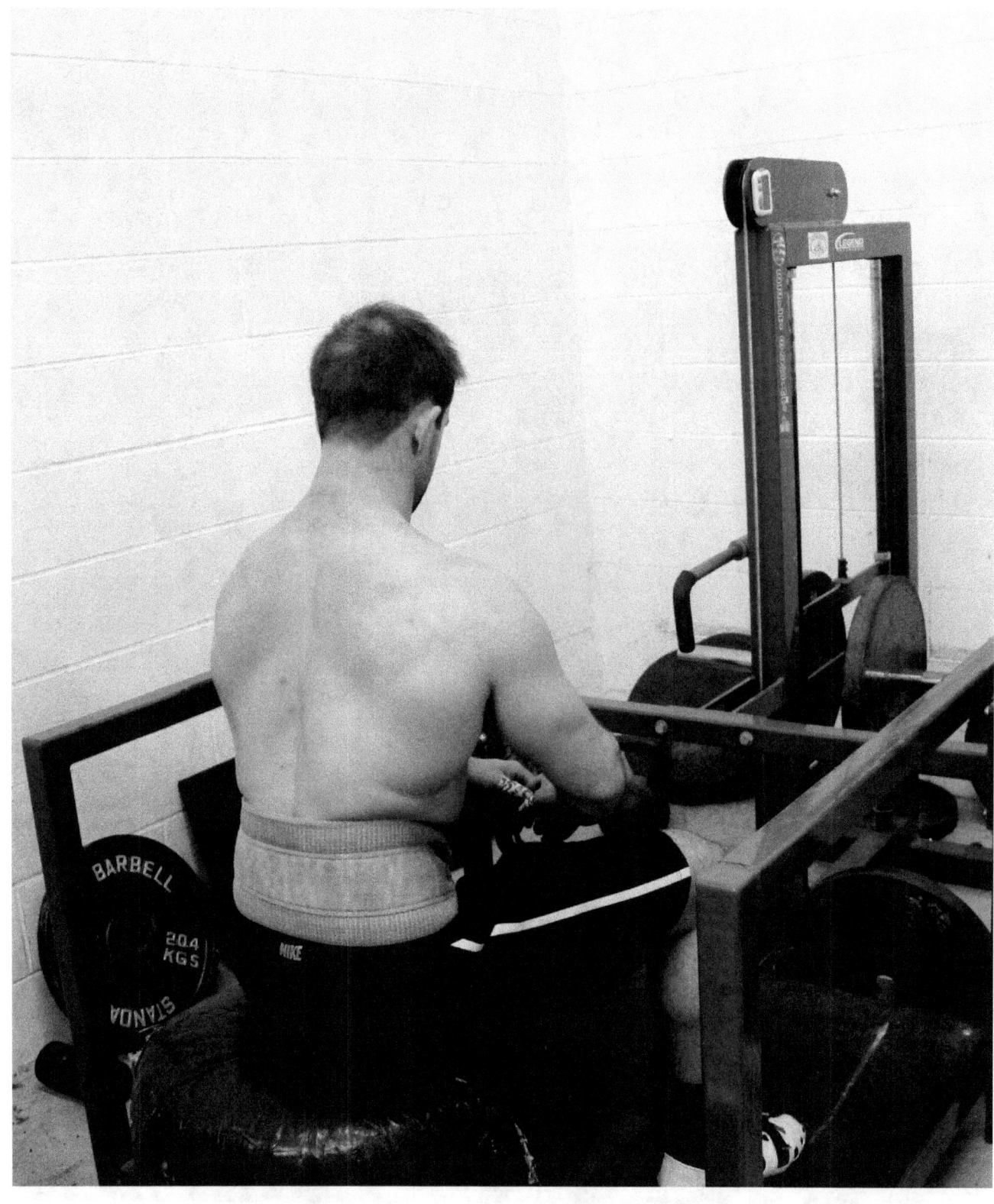

Belt Squats - B

Belt Squats - C

Belt Squats - D

Belt Squat Clean with Kettlebells - A

Belt Squat Clean with Kettlebells - B

Belt Squat Clean with Kettlebells - C

Belt Squat Clean with Kettlebells - D

Belt Squat Overhead Squat with Kettlebells - A

Belt Squat Overhead Squat with Kettlebells - B

Belt Squat Overhead Squat with Kettlebells - C

Belt Squat Overhead Squat with Kettlebells - D

Belt Squat Pull Through - Variation One - A

Belt Squat Pull Through - Variation One - B

Belt Squat Pull Through - Variation One - C

Belt Squat Pull Through - Variation Two-- A

Belt Squat Pull Through - Variation Two - B

Belt Squat Pull Through - Variation Two - C

Plyo Swings - A

Plyo Swings - B

Plyo Swings - C

Plyo Swings - D

Plyo Swings - E

Plyo Swings - F

Plyo Swing Leg Press - With Added Bands - A

Plyo Swing Leg Press - With Added Bands - B

Plyo Swing Leg Press - With Added Bands - C

Plyo Swing Leg Press - With Added Bands - D

Plyo Swing Leg Press - With Added Bands - E

Plyo Swing Leg Press - With Added Bands- F

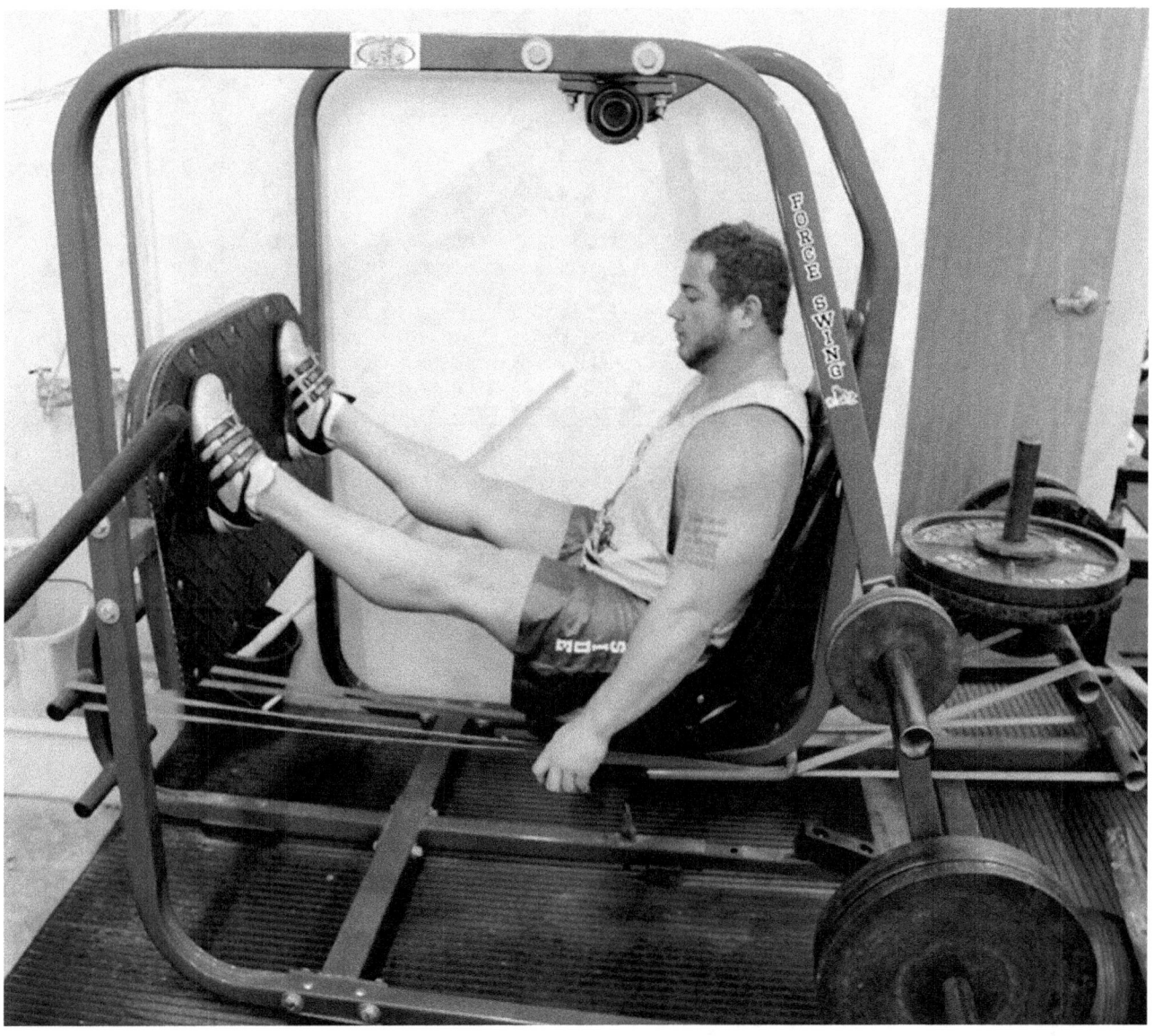

45-Degree Hyper - A

45-Degree Hyper - B

45-Degree Hyper - C

45-Degree Hyper - D

45-Degree Hyper - E

45-Degree Hyper - F

Back Attack - A

Back Attack - B

Back Attack - C

Back Attack - D

Back Attack - E

Back Attack - F

Hip Ab Developer - A

Hip Ab Developer - B

Lunge - A

Lunge - B

Lying Hamstring Curls - A

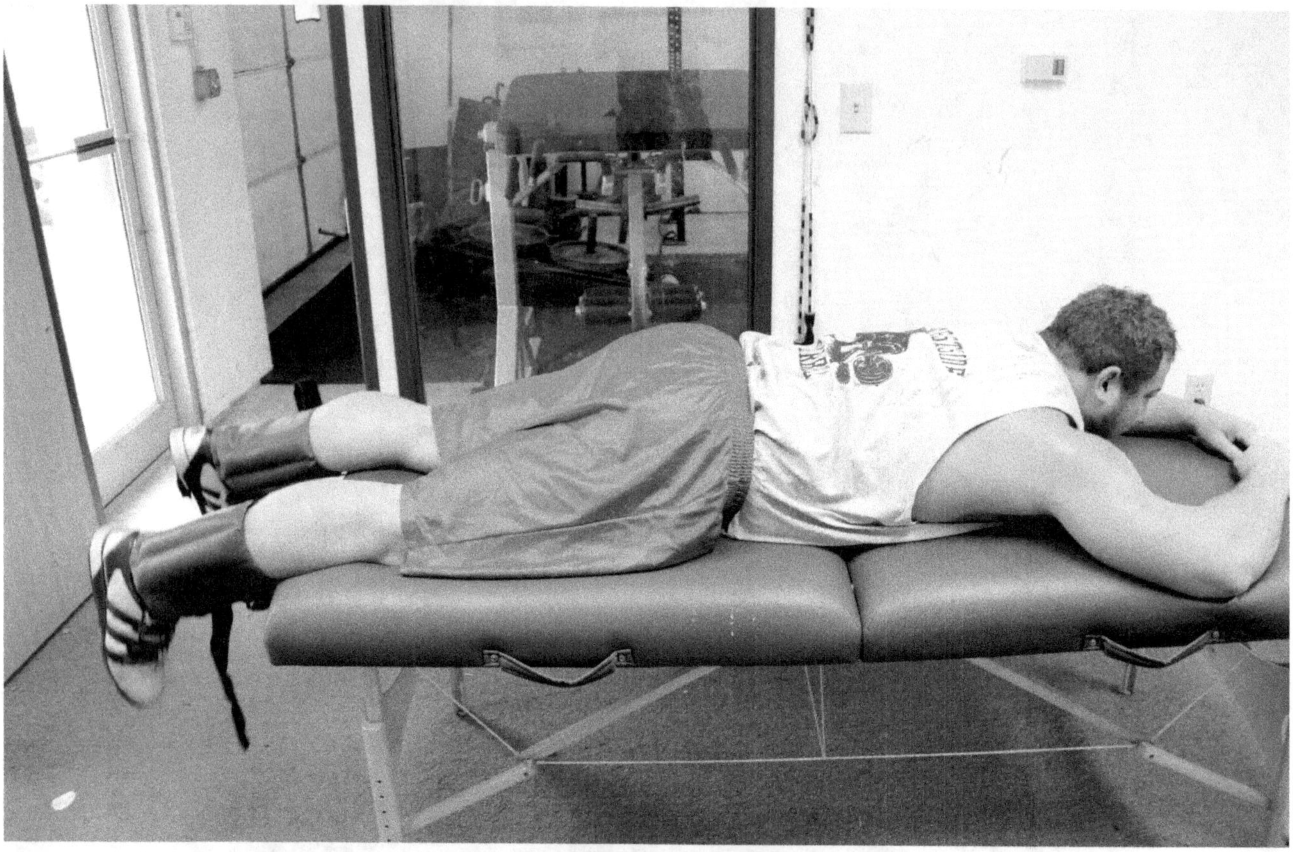

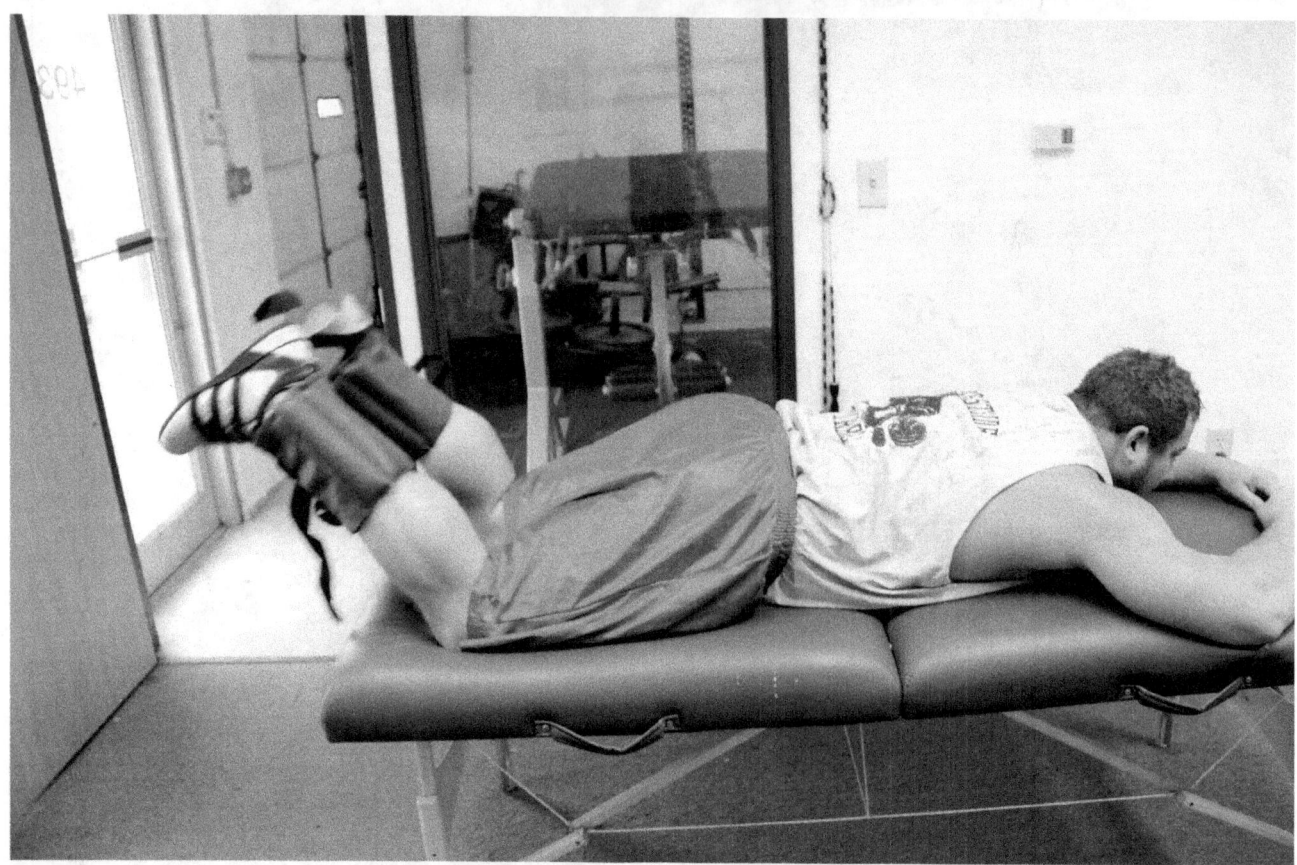

Lying Hamstring Curls - B

Lying Hamstring Curls - C

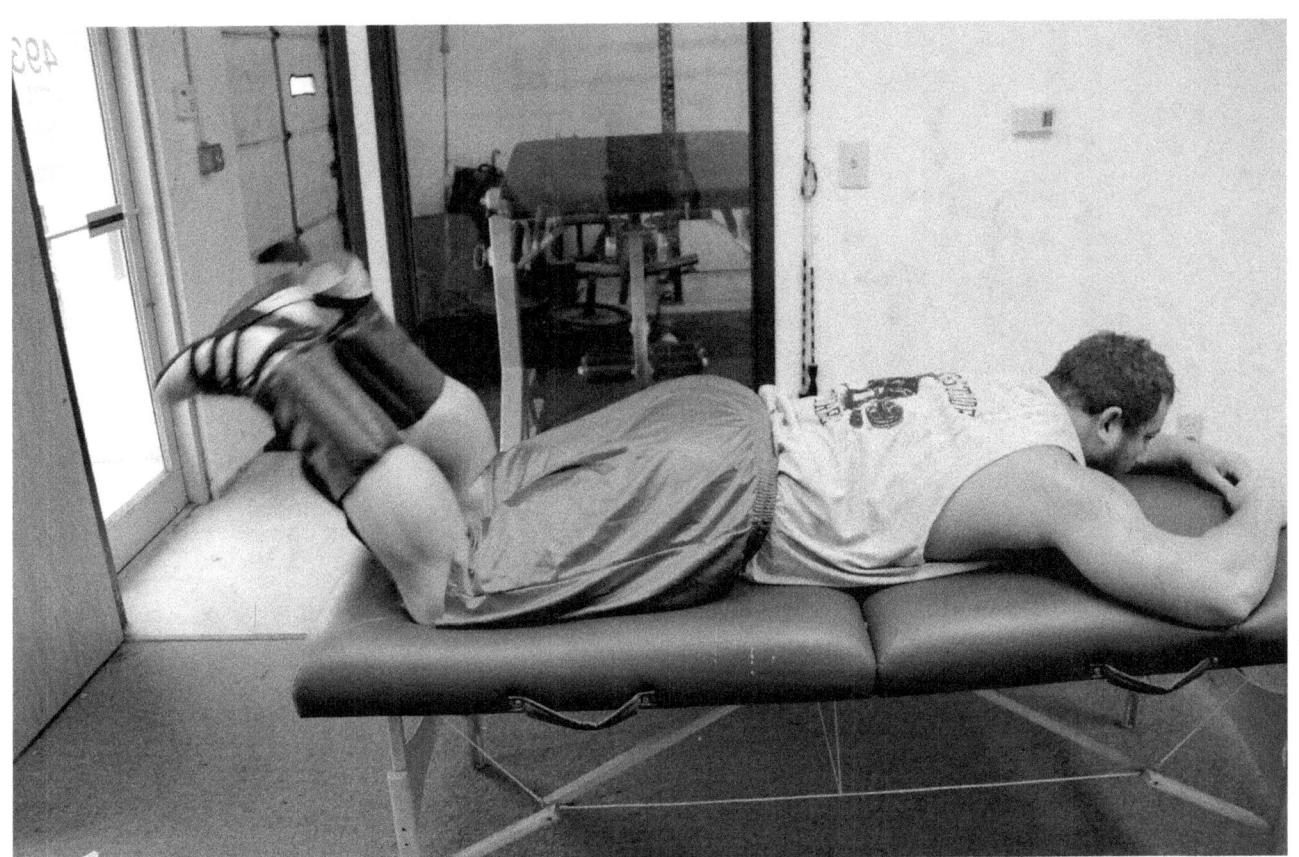

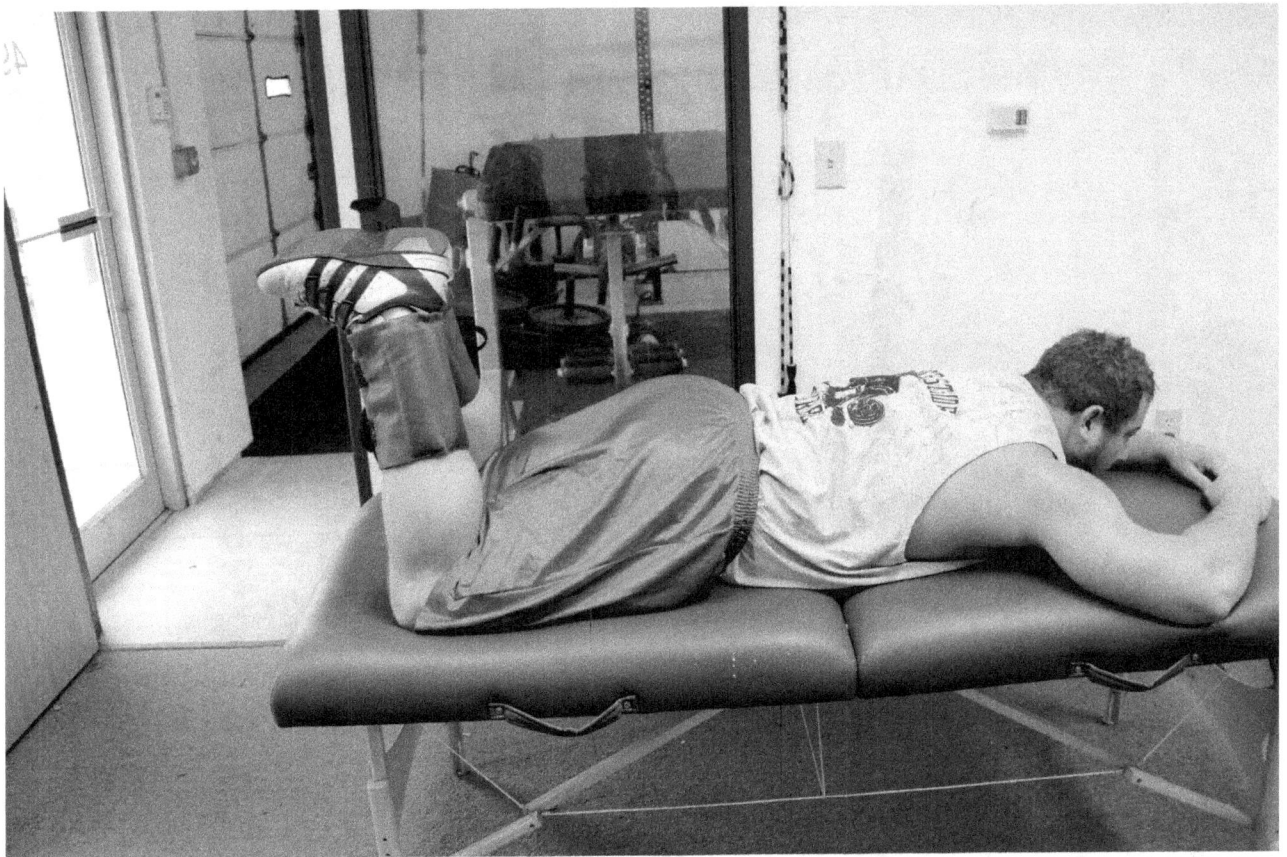

Lying Hamstring Curls - D

Lying Leg Raise - A

Lying Leg Raise - B

Lying Leg Raise - C

Lying Leg Raise - D

Pull Ups - A

Pull Ups - B

Reverse Hyper - A

Reverse Hyper - B

Side Bends - A

Side Bends - B

Single Leg Squat - A

Single Leg Squat - B

Standing Leg Curl - A

Standing Leg Curl - B

Triceps Extensions - A

Triceps Extensions - B

Triceps Extensions - C

Triceps Extensions - D

Triceps Extensions - E

Triceps Extensions - F

Williams Press - A

Williams Press - B

Williams Press - D

Selected Bibliography & References

Charniga, A. Weightlifting Technique and Training. Livonia, Mi.: Sportivny Press. (1992).

Dvorkin, L. Weightlifting and Age. Livonia Mi.: Sportivny Press. (1992).

Komi, P.V. Strength and Power in Sport. Great Britain, Blackwell Science Ltd. (1992).

Kurz, T. Science of Sports Training. Island Pont, VT: Stadion, (1990).

Laputin, N. & Oleshko V.G. Managing the Training of the Weightlifters.
Livonia Mi.: Sportivny Press. (1982).

Medvedev, A.S. A Program of Multi-Year Training in Weightlifting.
Livonia, Mi.: Sportivny Press. (1986).

Medvedev, A.S. A System of Multi-Year Training in Weightlifting.
Livonia, Mi.: Sportivny Press. (1989).

Roman R.A. The Training of the Weightlifter. Livonia Mi.: Sportivny Press, (1986)

Roman R.A. & Shakirzyanov M.S.
The Snatch, The Clean and Jerk. Fizkultura I Sport, Moscow (1978)

Siff, Mel C. Facts and Fallacies of Fitness. Denver Co.: Supertraining Institute, (2000).

Siff, M. Supertraining. Denver, Co.: Supertraining Institute, (2003).

Simmons, L. Westside Barbell Book of Methods. Ford du Lac, Wi: Action Printing, (2007)

Turkileri, E. Naim Suleymanoglu: The Pocket Hercules. Livonia Mi.: Sportivny Press, (2004).

Verkhoshansky, V.M. Fundamentals of Special Strength Training in Sports.
Livonia Mi.: Sportivny Press, (1997)

Verkhoshansky, Y.V. Programming and Organization of Training.
Livonia Mi.: Sportivny Press, (1985).

Viru, Atko. Adaptation in Sports Training. (1995).

Weightlifting Yearbook. A. Charniga, Trans. Livonia Mi.: Sportivny Press, (1985).

Weightlifting Yearbook. A. Charniga, Trans. Livonia Mi.: Sportivny Press, (1983).

Weightlifting Yearbook. A. Charniga, Trans. Livonia Mi.: Sportivny Press, (1981).

Weightlifting Yearbook. A. Charniga, Trans. Livonia Mi.: Sportivny Press, (1980).

Yessis, M. Soviet Sports Review. Volume 19, Number 2 (1984).

Yessis, M. Soviet Sports Review. Volume 19, Number 3 (1984).

Yessis, M. Soviet Sports Review. Volume 20, Number 1 (1985).

Yessis, M. Soviet Sports Review. Volume 20, Number 2 (1985).

Yessis, M. Soviet Sports Review. Volume 20, Number 3 (1985).

Yessis, M. Soviet Sports Review. Volume 20, Number 4   *(1985).*
Yessis, M. Soviet Sports Review. Volume 21, Number 3   *(1986).*
Yessis, M. Soviet Sports Review. Volume 21, Number 4   *(1986).*
Yessis, M. Soviet Sports Review. Volume 22, Number 1   *(1987).*
Yessis, M. Soviet Sports Review. Volume 22, Number 2   *(1987).*
Yessis, M. Soviet Sports Review. Volume 22, Number 4   *(1988).*
Yessis, M. Soviet Sports Review. Volume 24, Number 1   *(1989).*
Zatsiorsky, V.M. Science and Practice of Strength Training. Champaign, IL: Human Kinetics,   *(1995).*

www.ingramcontent.com/pod-product-compliance
Lightning Source LLC
Chambersburg PA
CBHW060303010526
44108CB00042B/2622